"As someone who has lost a spouse, and as someone who counsels others who are grieving, I highly recommend this book to anyone who is going through a time of grief, or if you know someone who is grieving and want to know more about the grief process. Dan shares his own journey through grief and loss with authenticity and honesty, and captures wonderfully that the goal of grief is not just to survive it, but to grow through it!"

JEREMY HYDE
Ordained Minister and Grief Counselor
Hospice of Scotland County
Laurinburg, NC

Dan, you got it right! Your thoughtful introduction, 'Life is Fair,' is an important context for hope and understanding when grieving a loss. Your experience and writing are consistent with my many years of work with persons on the pilgrimage through grief.

The ten essential dimensions of grief you identify do not happen in stages or any particular sequence, and not just one at a time, as you point out. They 'tumble' in on us unannounced and when we least expect them. Anyone experiencing loss who has the good fortune to read *Living with Loss* will gain understanding of the dynamic process and see it as normal.

The 'Good Companions' identified after each section are also an excellent way of helping a person who is experiencing loss to identify understanding companions who are so important on the pilgrimage to a 'renewed life.' Caregivers as well as the bereaved can benefit from reading *Living with Loss*.

REV. KENNETH E. REED, PhD
Developer/Author of Healing Through Grieving: Learning to Live Again

"I devoured every word, pausing only long enough between thoughts to ponder how those words had actually hit the nail on the head of my life! Over the years I have read many books on this subject and have tried to transfer those thoughts into my seminars with people who were experiencing many kinds of losses. However, it wasn't until I read *Living with Loss* that I could finally transfer the losses in the book to the losses in my life. Thank you for verbalizing what I have been experiencing that I could not identify."

C. SMITH
Motivational Speaker

"At some point in life, all human beings suffer loss. To survive and move forward, it is crucial to develop a philosophical perspective that offers sustaining power during those inevitable moments. Dan Moseley has written an exceptional book pastorally designed to help people deal with their anger, their guilt, and their pain at such times—and to emerge from the experience of loss with grace. Writes Moseley, 'To live is to love. To love is to lose. To lose is to live.' It is the process of loss that brings light into life, expands life; it is a gift that opens the future and makes new life possible."

D. Duane Cummins
Visiting Scholar in History, Johns Hopkins University
President Emeritus, Bethany College

LIVING WITH LOSS

DAN MOSELEY

XYZZY PRESS

LIVING WITH LOSS

Published in Nashville, Tennessee, by Xyzzy Press. www.xyzzypress.com

Cover Design: Eveready Press, Nashville, TN | www.eveready-usa.com
Cover Photo: Deborah Moseley
Interior Design: Inside Out Design & Typesetting

Library of Congress Cataloging-in-Publication Data
Moseley, Dan.
    Living with loss / by Dan Moseley.
        p. cm.
    Summary: "Discovering new life through the losses of life"—Provided by publisher.
    ISBN-13: 978-1-60148-005-7 (tradepaper)
    ISBN-10: 1-60148-005-9 (tradepaper)
 1. Loss (Psychology)—Religious aspects—Christianity.   2. Life change events—Religious aspects—Christianity.   3. Consolation.   4. Bereavement—Religious aspects—Christianity.   5. Grief—Religious aspects—Christianity.   6. Spiritual formation.   I. Title.
    BV4509.3.M67 2007
    248.8'6–dc22

                                                                    2007021408

Printed in the United States of America
07 08 09 10 11   LSI   9 8 7 6 5 4 3 2 1

To Deborah

For her faithful love and encouragement

Contents

Contents

Acknowledgments

Thanks to all who have walked with me through my life. Thanks to all those friends and family, strangers and therapists who listened to me long enough that I woke up and discovered my life.

I am especially grateful to my colleagues at Christian Theological Seminary who gave me a place to discover myself through sharing with students the stories that shaped my ministry and life. I am grateful to all the church people, professional and nonprofessional, who invited me to talk with them about loss and its impact on growth. I am also grateful to the groups of people who were grieving losses of children and friends who invited me to share their journey. Through their grace I discovered that I was not alone.

I am deeply grateful to my wife, Deborah, for her confidence in me. It is not easy to live into the life you have been given. Deborah has been a loving and grace-filled companion to me as I have discovered new life.

Foreword

Had anyone asked me to describe myself in April of 2002, I would have used words like happy, lucky, even blessed. I worked as a writer and had published seven books and articles and short stories in many national publications. I also taught creative writing part-time. My husband and I had two children, eight-year-old Sam and five-year-old Grace. Both kids were healthy, funny, smart, and talented. We lived in a house in Providence, Rhode Island, that was built in 1792.

When we moved there in 1999, Grace dubbed it the Happy House, and indeed that moniker seemed true the warm Sunday that I pulled into our driveway from the airport. I was returning from the Virginia Festival of the Book in Charlottesville, and the sight of my family after four days away made me smile. There was Lorne putting chicken on the barbecue grill and Sam setting the table with the garish floral plates I had bought on sale. And there was Grace, watching for me. As soon as she saw me, she ran to our small garden and made me a bouquet of chives and myrtle. Grace brought me that bouquet, calling, "Mama's home! Mama's home!" as she ran toward me. Three days later, Grace was dead from a virulent form of strep. And my family was left stunned and heartbroken by the suddenness, the unfairness, the horror of our loss.

In the past, reading and writing had always brought me comfort and solace. Even as a young child, books and words helped me to work out my problems, ease heartaches, understand the world around me. Suddenly, they abandoned me. I lost Grace and my ability to find solace in the only places I knew. Grieving people get angry—at God, at people around them, at the world that can rob them yet still continue to spin. My husband sought and found help in our church, a Congregational one with a minister our own age and an assistant minister with a penchant for guitar playing and mischief. Our family had been active church members; Lorne and I attended church and potluck suppers, fundraisers and sandwich brigades. Sam and Grace both performed in the Christmas pageant every year and sat at the assistant minister's feet during Children's Hour.

For me, these familiar touchstones brought pain rather than comfort. Our ministers' admission of a lack of answers to help understand our tragedy sent me away from, rather than toward, the church. Lorne and I, desperate for help, visited clergy of other faiths as well. We sat in the offices of rabbis and priests, seeking answers. Of course, there were none. But somehow I held on to the belief—the hope—that one of these people of faith would give me something to ease my pain, a spiritual salve of sorts. Too often the clergyperson would glance at his or her watch, then dismiss us with a stale platitude: time heals. Or: you will feel better someday. Or: it isn't our job to understand these things. Each disappointing meeting sent Lorne back to our church, our ministers. And each sent me farther from any faith, in fact, farther from God.

As time passed and Lorne returned to work and Sam to school, the terrible feeling that perhaps I no longer even believed in God began to creep into my mind. The idea terrified me. Raised a Catholic in an Italian family, God was ever present. We didn't question his existence no matter what happened to us. Organized religion was secondary in our household; faith and belief in God was mandatory. Sometimes it would hit me: *I don't believe in God!* and I would gasp. As I watched Lorne embrace church and its community, my own realization became more horrible to me.

I kept returning to a day just a week before Grace died. The weather was unusually warm, the sun bright and yellow. I dropped Sam at his school, and then Grace and I sang along with the Beatles' *Help!* album on the way to the montessori school where she attended kindergarten. We performed our usual routine of hugging and kissing at the door, with Grace commanding: "Hug! Hug! Kiss!" until she disappeared inside, her oversized backpack banging. I got back in the car and became overwhelmed with a feeling of gratitude for all that I had. A prayer of thanks ran through my head: *Thank you, God, for these beautiful children, this wonderful life.* So strong was this feeling that I actually grew teary and repeated the little prayer out loud.

When Grace died, that moment came back to me with full

force. Would the God I had given such heartfelt thanks to, take Grace from me? How could there be a God if this was how the world worked? Devastated, I slowly came to the conclusion that there was no God. How could there be?

Somehow that summer after Grace died, I decided to keep my commitment to teach writing at the Chautauqua Institute in western New York. Coincidentally, Dan Moseley was there, giving daily sermons. His topic was grief, and I found myself drawn to those sermons, and to Dan himself. In those still raw days of grieving, I acted desperately. I wailed in supermarket aisles. I threw myself on the ground in pain. I cried endlessly. When I approached Dan to speak to him, I started to cry uncontrollably. But he remained calm and steady. We set up a time to meet that afternoon.

What Dan gave me that day, and what he offers throughout this book, was what everyone who suffers loss of any kind needs. He listened without judgment. He allowed me to cry. He did not even once look at his watch. When I stood, aware that an hour had passed, he looked surprised. "Where are you going?" he asked. Then he gave me his e mail address. That address became a lifeline for me during months of sleepless, grief-filled nights. I always knew that someone who cared was on the other end.

For all of these reasons, I was able to say out loud to Dan what I had not been able to utter: I don't think I believe in God anymore. He did not look angry, or shocked, or upset. He simply nodded. This questioning, this doubt, was acceptable, even appropriate! I was not, Dan helped me to realize, the same person I used to be. I was now a mother without a daughter; a woman grieving an enormous, unspeakable loss; a writer without words. Dan's gifts to me were many. His lessons essential. And perhaps the most important was to help me understand that I needed to re-define myself. Who was I without Grace? What could I make of this new life? How did God and faith fit into it?

Now, five years later, my life has taken new and unexpected shapes. Lorne and I adopted a baby girl, Annabelle, from China in 2005. I have found my words again and have written a new novel, *The Knitting Circle*. I have learned to knit, and do so voraciously. I do all of these things yet can still carry Grace with me. Moving on isn't moving away from your loved ones.

About God, I still have not reconciled my anger and hurt with who I thought God was. But now I allow myself to explore those feelings and thoughts. I allow myself to look at the peonies in all their glory in my yard, my son Sam growing into a young man, the sweet kiss of my husband, the joy of Annabelle—all of these gifts and more—and I can finally think: maybe there is a God.

Of course, everyone's journey through loss and grief is different. However, I feel confident that you will find comfort in these pages. You will find courage and companionship and wisdom. And, dare I say, you will even find hope, a glimpse of something sublime that exists even amid the cruelest loss.

Ann Hood
June 2007

Prologue

This book is for you if you've ever lost a lover, a friend, a dog, a job, a partner, a championship game, a leg, an eye, a baby, a dream, a breast, a house, a car, a business.

And it is for you if you have ever wondered what good people can do when bad things happen to them.

And it is for you if your city of residence, your job, your family structure, your school, your physical ability, your beliefs, or your worldview has ever changed.

And it is for you if you have ever traveled to other cultures, become acquainted with strangers, had a baby, been betrayed, gotten married, or gotten divorced.

If any of these things have happened to you, this book is for you because this is a book on discovering new life through the losses of life.

You see, each of these events, and any other event that happens to create a significant change in your self-understanding, results in the experience of loss. Whether we choose the change or not, each change produces loss. If we get married, we lose our single life. If we get pregnant, we lose our sense of independence. If our lover dies, we lose our sense of being loved.

And a lot more. This book is a book about the multilayered losses we experience in the living of our lives.

Moreover, this book is about what people do in the face of these changes and losses that results in some amazing and wonderful discoveries. It is about how loss is the central component in our desire to discover new dimensions of ourselves. It is about how the creation of space caused by change is exactly what is needed if we are going to become more than we have been.

While this is a book about loss and the sadness that accompanies our losses, it is also about the discovery of more life and the excitement and adventure of that discovery.

If you are looking for a book on how you can do more to make these losses less painful or how to avoid them altogether, this is not a book for you. This is not a book to show you how you are living your life in the wrong way, and that if you would just change yourself, you would be better. Books like that just produce guilt. They make us feel more inadequate than we already feel and do not contribute to living our strength and confidence through these losses.

This book is not a list of stages or steps you must follow in your journey through loss. There is no right way to do this any more than there is just one right way to live your life. This life is your life. And there is no straight line from here to there. When we think life is a series of steps that, if we just step rightly, we will get what we want and have no pain, we start making judgments on ourselves from the beginning. If someone says we should be at stage three after four months of missing the husband who left us, and we are only at stage one, we not only have to deal with our feelings, but we deal with our guilt for not being where we ought to be. One of the most painful things about grieving loss is our expectations and the expectations of others, which make us feel we are not doing it right.

This book is not about doing it right. This book is about living life through the losses of life. This is an invitation to follow the scenic route through life, to pay attention to your life, to notice what is happening and, as you do, to receive it as a gift. For the road of our lives is one in which there are wanderings, roads that double back on themselves, allowing us to revisit old sites even as we wind our way toward new sights. This is an invitation to wake up to your life, to live your life as you go, to love your life as you experience it.

This is not a book with answers. It is a book with clues that come from my life and the lives of people I know. Someone has said that if the path ahead is clear, it is not your path. Your life is a mystery. No one can give you all the answers. But when we share honestly with each other, we glean hints from one another about what might be our way. I will give you my honest experience and hope that it will illumine your path.

Come with me on a journey of discovery. I will share with you what I found in my painful experiences of loss and the joyful and graceful life that emerges through that loss. I will share with you what my friends have shared with me as we have walked together through change. I heard somewhere we read to know that we are not alone. I share with you these stories with the hope that on your journey, you will know you are not alone.

I invite you to allow your own heart to open up to others so that you can find fresh joy in these new discoveries. I encourage you to share your journey so that those who feel your sadness can drink from your joy as they walk with you.

Introduction: Life Is Fair

Someone once said, "Life after all is fair. Ultimately it breaks everybody's heart."[1]

I would have thought I would have known this. After all, I spent over thirty years sharing the pain and joy of life with people in three congregations. As their pastor, I had spent countless hours walking alongside hundreds of people as they experienced all that life had to offer. I shared the agony of divorce with them, wept with them as they gave up their wife to death, swore at the gods with them as they mourned the death of their little baby, descended into the depths with them as they were fired after twenty-four years with their company. I would have thought I'd have known that eventually life breaks everyone's heart.

Ironically it took far more for me to get that through my thick skin. I had to be stripped of the insulation that protected me from the pain. I had to be confronted with more loss and death than I could handle. It began with the discovery of cancer and, three years later, the death of my first wife, Cindy. We had been married thirty-one years. Soon thereafter, the young custodian of the church I was serving took his lover and her children hostage and then, before the night was over, he had killed his lover and himself. Then the last of my three children got married and moved out. A month later my dad died.

Now, I was accomplished at facing difficulty with other people. My role as minister gave me a way of being present to the pain without it cutting so deep. But when the losses began to pile up and rip through my self-understanding as a husband, a father, and a son, I was without enough resources to keep on going.

I continued to do my work as a preacher and pastor, but I found it more and more difficult. Speaking words of meaning became hollow. I felt like a "noisy gong and a clanging symbol." When I visited people in the hospital, I got physically sick. I found more and more ways to avoid confronting the issues of leadership that were my job.

Finally, I chose to leave the congregation that had mentored and nurtured me and that I had served for over twenty years. I chose to leave the profession of pastor that had sustained me and given me identity for over thirty years. I decided to leave the city in which I had discovered my skills as a minister and offered them as a gift to others. I chose to lose much more after facing losses over which I had no choice.

It was only then that the full impact of the losses of my life came crashing in. As I moved to a new city and became a professor at a seminary, I began to spin into chaos. As the relationships which had sustained me through the crises of my life ended, I was left naked and on my own. I could no longer avoid my feelings. I could no longer pretend that life would be the same. I discovered the terror of not knowing who I was.

And I discovered real empathy. Susan Wiltshire, in her book about her brother dying from AIDS, describes a broken heart like a broken biscuit. When it is torn in half, there is twice as much surface on which to spread the butter and honey.[2] I discovered that there is also twice as much surface on which to spread the pain and grief of others. Whereas I was able to protect my heart by playing the role of pastor, I now had no such protection. While I was able to draw on the strength that people projected on me because I was a "man of God," now I was just Dan. I had no presence to offer but my own. And the pain that others felt tore into my flesh as well.

It was then I began to realize the truth of the statement: Life is fair. Eventually it breaks everyone's heart.

I found that our hearts are attached to familiar, dependable relationships and that when these change, by accident or choice (it matters not), the heart gets ripped apart.

It was in the midst of this that I began to reflect on my own journey—to discover if there was anything in this grieving that could help me understand and live life better. My heart had cracked open and the wounds of loss were raw. Sadness consumed me. I wanted comforting, warm light to anoint the wounds and heal me. Let the suffering ease and hope visit my heart again. I wanted to believe there was light coming in through the cracks of my heart, but I didn't know how to get through the pain to discover the light.

As I looked at what I was doing with my life, I realized the truth of the poet Jack Gilbert, who said, "We must unlearn the constellations to see the stars."[3] I realized the life I had created was no longer the life I could live. I had learned a particular way of naming reality. The people and actions of my life were constructed in a particular way and created constellations by which I named them. The constellations were named husband, pastor, father, and son. As life's structures disappeared, I was unable to name myself and was left looking at a black sky with millions of stars. I could no longer see the constellations—just the stars.

Dim Lights

I found myself slowing down because I didn't know who I was anymore. When I experienced the loss of my wife, my dad, my job, and the community I had called home, someone turned off the lights in my life. When you can't see very well, you don't move as fast.

But the lights don't go off all of a sudden. Sometimes when there is a painful loss, there is a sudden burst of bright light. After a person has lost a spouse, I often hear people ask, "How's she doing?"

During the first week or so, the answer to the question is: "She is doing amazingly well. She's taking care of business."

Painful loss often produces a spurt of energy and clarity which one seldom experiences in the normal routine of life. Adrenaline rushes through our system, which insulates us from the pain and energizes us to endure the stress produced by the loss.

For most of us though, that light begins to dim near the time that our energy runs out. The energy required to deal with the immediate need to simply hold on and create some temporary stability is soon depleted. The clarity provided by the immediate tasks soon fades as the fog of unknowing descends upon us. We often find ourselves sleeping much more than we did before. The dark of sleep is much more welcoming than the light of reality that faces us.

This slowing down is very much related to the inability to see where we are going. It is very much like the descending sunset and the emerging dark of night. We find ourselves drawn to the immediacy of the present by the palpable pain of emptiness and fear. We have known the way when the person we lost was still living with us, even if the way was tough. But when they are gone, we have a much harder time deciding where we are going.

Fran was married for fifteen years. Several times during the marriage, Fran was physically abused by her husband. Despite the abuse, she stayed with him because she loved him and believed the stability of the marriage was best for her and her children. She knew how to make it through most of the days and years without suffering abuse. She walked on eggshells, but she walked nonetheless. She knew if she avoided certain topics and gave in when he got angry, she would be okay.

However, one night the abuse became so brutal Fran decided she had had enough. She was terrorized by her husband and she was terrorized by leaving her husband. But she finally found the courage to leave.

The freedom Fran felt when she left was almost as frightening as the terror she feared from her husband. How could she live? How could she provide support for her children? How could she be a single parent? Darkness descended and Fran did not know what to do. The energy she had mustered to leave her husband had now evaporated and she was depressed, exhausted. It felt to Fran that someone had turned out the lights.

Reorienting in the Dark

When the lights go out and we are unable to see clearly where we are going, we slow down. We sometimes stop. We try to get oriented. Because the eyes do not pick up signals that help us know where we are, we often use our other senses. We reach out our hand, feeling our way along. We listen, trying to determine if there is something that sounds familiar. Our sense of smell stretches up on tip-toe trying to detect something that can give us a sense of where we are.

I remember hiking in the woods several years ago. Initially I was following trails others had made but I eventually began to feel adventurous, wanting to discover unexplored areas. I took off through the underbrush. I was sure I would come across another trail. But as the sun started to set, I was hopelessly lost. I began to feel anxiety because I was losing my sight in the dimming light. I saw nothing that gave me a clue as to where I was. Then I realized I was seeing deer droppings. I realized deer had been on the narrow path I was following. I also listened and heard in the distance automobile traffic. I knew the road went north and therefore I was walking west. My senses helped orient me and I soon found my way back to the trail and returned to my car.

When it is dark, we slow down and use other senses to find our way.

Slowing Down

When we lose someone or some activity, we slow down to a speed that feels safe. Each step is a cautious effort. Someone once told me that they experienced the loss of their mother as a descending dark. They said they had to live as if they were driving at night. They could only go as fast as their headlights would allow them to see.

When we have lost someone, it is helpful to remember that we are in the dark and our eyes have to adjust. It helps to remember that our friends may be offering a flashlight of encouragement to help us see a little farther ahead, but these are their flashlights and not ours. The future in the dark is often seen only as a vague outline. When we are driving at night without lights, it is often hard to tell if what is ahead of us is a dog or a shadow. The uncertainty of what we see means we move cautiously, in spite of our own desire or the desire of others that we move more quickly.

Moving forward in the dark is deceptive and often confusing. Sometimes we think we see clearly, and other times we are certain we don't see anything at all. When my wife Deborah and I first started dating, we were both in freefall. Deborah was adjusting to being single after a divorce that ended a twenty-five year marriage. I was adjusting to single life after losing my wife to death, my career to a job change, and my home of twenty years. When Deborah and I first began to date, we saw clearly and the passion was palpable. We saw clearly by the burning passion. Then one of us would get scared, and the night of uncertainty would envelop us and we would back away from the relationship. This occurred a couple of times over a three-year period. Eventually the darkness of fear and uncertainty gave way to more consistent light and we decided to move ahead together. We began to make plans farther down the road than simply the impulse of the moment. We began to wake up not only to our present feelings and fears but also to the dreams and hopes that light the path into the future.

Back Roads

Another way of looking at this process of waking to the light is to imagine that the losses of our life slow us down so we might travel the back roads of our souls. In his book *Immortality*, Milan Kundera helped me see the connection between my exploring the back roads of the United States and the journey of my soul.

Since I had begun to experience the life-shredding losses of my life, I had avoided interstates and major highways whenever I could. I took the back roads to work, to visit my mother, and to travel across the country.

In his novel, Kundera believes there is a difference between roads and highways.

A highway differs from a road not only because it is solely intended for vehicles, but also because it is merely a line that connects one point with another. A highway has no meaning in itself; its meaning derives entirely from the two points it connects. A road is a tribute to space. Every stretch of road has meaning in itself and invites us to stop. A highway is the triumphant devaluation of space, which thanks to it has been reduced to a mere obstacle to human movement and a waste of time.

He continues,

Before roads and paths disappeared from the landscape, they had disappeared from the human soul: man stopped wanting to walk, to walk on his own feet and enjoy it. What's more, he no longer saw his life as a road, but as a highway: a line that led from one point to another, from the rank of captain to the rank of general, from the role of wife to the role of widow. Time became a mere obstacle to life, an obstacle that had to be overcome by ever greater speed.[4]

Kundera spoke to the deep desire I discovered to slow down and to allow life to be lived in me. I had spent much of my life getting from point A to point B, and was living at such a furious speed, I failed to notice life along the road. The external journey from the highways to the back roads was a response to my soul's desire to find life in the journey rather than at some destination.

As I traveled the back roads of my soul, I came to discover rich insights into living life more fully. I discovered there are experiences that occur to us, and whether we want them to happen or not, they can be gifts of life to us. I discovered loss is the one fundamental thing in life you can count on.

Change and Loss

Change is the one truth about reality that is incontrovertible. If something is alive, it is changing. And if something is changing, something is dying. I have discovered that loss is a gift that opens up the future in ways nothing else can. It is the way new life is possible.

Now this is a very difficult perspective to sell in our society. Our culture actually believes that winning is everything. One of the worst things a person can be called is a loser. Our culture is enchanted with the winners, the celebrities, the people who are on top. But we are simultaneously cruel and callous toward those who were on top and then fall. The message of this book, that we lose our way to life, is not easy to sell. However, it is a word of truth and hope for those ordinary people who live life in its fullness. It makes sense to those who have experienced what life delivers to all—the experience of losing something that is core to who we see ourselves to be.

Mantra

I was speaking at a national gathering and asked to share my spiritual journey in eight minutes. Accepting the challenge, I boiled down my life and realized that my spiritual journey could be summed up in the following mantra: To live is to love. To love is to lose. To lose is to live.

In looking back at my life, I realized that love is what creates life. What we love makes us who we are. If we love words, we become someone who lives with words. If we love baseball, we will spend time playing or watching it because it makes us feel alive. If we love our children, we will spend our lives being the kind of parent who loves children. What we love gives us life.

But to love is to lose. We love that which is created, and we are created by that which we love. We love people. We love things. We love ourselves at a particular time in our lives. We loved high school. We loved that dress. We loved being a mother nursing our baby. If we love our children, we become a person who is a parent to the children. We shape our life according to what the love of a child demands of us. If we love our job, we become one who is shaped by the job. We love created things. And because we love what is not permanent, we are guaranteed to lose. Because we love what is in a state of constant change, we will lose what we know as we know it.

Because change is the fundamental nature of life, we will lose what we love. That is assured. We love our job, but eventually we will lose that job—either because we lose our love for what we are doing or because someone more qualified gets our job or because we retire from our job or we die doing our job. At some point, what we lose and what makes us know that we are alive will disappear. To love is to lose.

We become who we are by what we love. When we lose what we love, we lose part of who we are. When our husband walks out on us after twenty years of marriage, we are no longer who we were. Sometimes we have become so shaped by the way love was expressed for the partner that we lose a very significant part of ourselves. Our sadness and pain is therefore as much for the loss of ourselves as it is for the loss of the other.

To live is to love. To love is to lose. But to lose is to live. If we lose one part of our life, we are open to another part. If we love having young children at home and then they grow up and leave home, the empty space created by their leaving opens the door to love something else—like loving the freedom to travel or visit with adults without interruption. When something disappears, it opens the space for something else.

My granddaughter is six years old. As her baby teeth fall out, she smiles her toothless smile. She was scared when the first one fell out, but her fear eased when she put it under her pillow and received money from the tooth fairy. And now she is proud—new teeth are coming in. And she is excited about the new teeth. Her fear fades as she grows in the confidence that new teeth will take the place of the ones that are lost. Had she not lost those teeth, there would not have been room for new teeth. To lose is to live.

For this new growth to happen, ten dimensions must be experienced. Each one will occur in its own time. These are not steps that one takes, one after another. They are dimensions of a process that all who grow through loss experience, consciously or unconsciously.

And this process has two names: grieving and spiritual growth.

Growing Through Grieving

To grieve is to learn to live again in the absence of someone or something significant. It isn't just the time of unbearable emptiness and tears. It is the whole process of becoming a new person who is shaped by the memory of what is lost, not defined by it. It is becoming a person who has experienced a divorce, not a divorced person. It is becoming a person who has lost a partner, not being a widow. It is becoming a person who has experienced the loss of a job, not a fired person. It is knowing ourselves as persons who lose when change occurs, not people who are losers.

And therefore grieving is something that takes time. It is not an easy process if the loss for which one grieves represents a defining reality in your life. The amount of time it takes is related to the depth of the loss. When a young man loses an important conference game, he will go through this process relatively quickly. The process is the way he attends to the pain of the loss and then becomes free of the pain so it doesn't define how he will play the next game later in the week. He will be shaped by the loss but not controlled by it. The woman whose husband dies the year before he retires takes longer to discover the new life through this process of grieving and growing. Her identity and self-understanding have developed over forty years and the losses will be more complex and multidimensional.

The process of grieving is painful because it is a birthing process. It is a stretching and tearing that opens the way for a new spirit to emerge. It requires the knitting together of painful and pleasant memories to discover a new way of understanding ourselves.

As I worked on this process in my own life, I did a great deal of reading and study of spirituality and growth. And I came to realize that the process of grieving loss, of learning to live in the absence of someone or something significant, is a parallel process to what many religions call a spiritual pilgrimage. To grow spiritually isn't simply the practice of reading about the good ideas of others, but it is about the way we process the changes in our lives. It is about the way we walk from death to life as we move from what is lost to what is yet to love. Spiritual growth in religious circles is about living through a breaking, stretching, aching, remaking process of letting go of that which is gone and taking on a life that is formed in response to what is coming to be.

Death and Rebirth

In the home of my childhood, words were king. I was fed words with my mother's milk and learned to relish them. I learned to trust them. As I learned to speak, I was constantly reminded how to speak correctly. I learned there were words that built up and words that tore down. If I used words that tore down (telling my brother he was "stupid," for instance), I paid a high price. If I used words that my mother felt demeaned the human enterprise (like "damn" or "hell"), I was required to go pick my own switch and roll up my pant legs. I became a student, and spoken and printed words fed my mind. I became a singer, and poetic words dressed in notes became my soul's food.

After the series of deaths that invaded my life over a decade ago, however, words died. I lost words. I lost my voice. I realized that words are like dust—cast to the wind and scattered, seldom having the lasting impact one desires.

The result was my inability to read or write. I lost the focus necessary to follow a sentence across the page and hold its meaning in my mind. I tried writing but could not develop any confidence in it. When I spoke in public, I felt tentative—stumbling and qualifying.

I came to realize that the mind in chaos has a hard time taking words into itself and ordering them into any sense. Because my mind couldn't process the way it was accustomed to, I discovered I was much more in touch with my body and my soul. My heart was also too confused and I couldn't stay in relationships very well. I realized these losses had effectively driven me out of my mind and into my body, out of my heart and into my soul.

After several years of struggle, I was surprised by a discovery which has resulted in my being free to put these words down on a page and send them out to others in a book. I was hiking in the forest that has become my playground. I sat one crisp fall day on a bench looking at what I call the broccoli tree. (It looks like a hundred-foot stalk of broccoli.) As the last of the late-autumn leaves drifted to the ground, I had a deep sense of sadness. I realized the leaves were much like the words I had spoken most of my life. They had fallen from my lips and turned brown. The smell of decay was in the air. I realized that most of the words by which I had made my living had long ago disintegrated. They were not remembered, nor were they framed and put on a wall.

As I was pondering this process, I settled into a deep sense of contentment. Yes, the leaves fall and die. Yes, the words fall on people's ears and die. But the decaying leaves become the humus that nourishes the tree and becomes the fertile home for the gestation of new seedlings. Maybe that is what words do—they are not to live forever. They are simply designed to fall and die and silently and perpetually fertilize the new life that emerges from the earth.

As I was coming to this understanding, I was released from my block and decided I could write again. Then as I was relaxing in the crisp fall sun, an acorn fell and struck me right on top of my head. All the fluttering, descending leaves had spoken so gently and then suddenly, one hard little acorn dropped from nowhere and made its point. Only a few words make an impact. The rest do their work of decay and death and becoming humus for the nurturing of new life.

This book is hopefully both brown leaves and hard acorns. It is a result of the journey from trust and confidence in the life I had been given, the collapse of that life, and the emergence of new life and understanding.

This book is about those ten dimensions of reality we experience as we learn to embrace the new and leave the old. It is about the experience of rebirth that is the gift that comes to those who pay attention to their life and who have the courage and patience to discover the gifts that are a part of losing, loving, and living.

As the ten dimensions of experience common to loss are identified, you are invited to recognize them in your own journey, to attend to your feelings and your thoughts as you experience them. You are encouraged to slow down and explore the gifts that come through these experiences. I believe that when you do, you will find new parts of yourself and new resources for living a rich and vital life in the future.

In this book we will also identify persons who might be companions for your journey. As you explore these parts of your own life, you will want to seek out friends who can walk with you. You need several. No one person can be all things to you. Sometimes you need intimate friends, sometimes you need strangers. I have discovered that the presence of multiple companions helps us live these experiences more fully. They can help us discover new parts of ourselves that we might miss were we to walk alone. And when you yourself walk with others through these experiences, you can help them grow in spirit and life if you attend to some of these ways of being present with them.

Welcome to the journey. Welcome to the pilgrimage. Welcome to the discovery of life.

Naming the Loss

To learn to live again in the absence of someone or something that is gone requires that one develop the ability to *name that which is lost*. Now, that may seem like a simple assignment. After all, when someone dies, it is clear what is lost. She is no longer here. She has stopped breathing. She has stopped talking. She has stopped touching.

When you lose a job, it is clear what is lost. You are no longer getting paid to get in your car and drive to an office and do some task that satisfies a need of some organization.

When you lose a partner, it is clear what you have lost. He is no longer coming home at night. He is no longer there to talk with you. He is no longer there affirming you or comforting you.

But it's not always so obvious. The fact is, most significant losses are multilayered. Most of us are unable to name all the losses immediately. If we did, it would be so overwhelming we could not stand it. When my dad died, he physically disappeared from my life. That was about all I could deal with at the beginning. I could not talk with him on the phone. I could not hear his wry humor and his shy laughter. I could not smell his aroma. I could not call to get his advice.

After some time went by, I realized I had lost a constancy I could not describe. I realized there was an empty space that his death had created in me. I realized there were some answers to questions I would never get. I could ask my mother about what Daddy did and what he felt, but, I would never really get his answers.

And then more time expired and I realized I had lost my buffer. He was no longer there to protect me from my own mortality. I could no longer assume I would live forever because there was still someone there who would have to die first. But now he was gone. I would be next.

Sue lost her partner in parenting. They were parents of small children. When her partner died, she was left alone. Along with the agony of an empty bed, she experienced the losses of companionship, friendship, and planning. The person whom she had bounced ideas off of was not there anymore.

In time, she also began to feel another loss. She discovered her confidence in parenting was not nearly as strong. She discovered she had only known herself as a partnered parent. She had never known herself as a single parent.

Her children were acting differently as well. They had never known her as a single parent. They had only known the parenting that was done together. So they had lost a sense of safety and security they had known with both parents.

Then a third loss soon emerged. Sue realized she didn't trust life to sustain her in the future. She saw how fragile life was. She saw there was no guarantee and that life can be very short. Because of this discovery, she found

> *When we lose the future, it is hard to know what to do in the present. Loss of the future causes us to wonder if there is anything worth planning or living for.*

herself fluctuating between conserving everything, trying to hold on to the things she had, and spending everything since there was no future to save for.

When someone we love dies, we discover the future we had known is gone. When we lose the future, it is hard to know what to do in the present. Loss of the future causes us to wonder if there is anything worth planning or living for; it all seems to come to nothing.

Sue also discovered that the music of her life with her partner was no longer being written. They had played, laughed, cried, struggled, traveled, and lived together for seventeen years. Now her partner was no longer there to contribute to her music. Sue felt she was left to finish the unfinished symphony alone. She had to find some kind of resolution to the harmony and discord, which was characterized by the music of their lives. Writing the symphony alone when you have always done it with another is a difficult and fearful thing to do. You want to write it in a way that has the integrity of the one who is gone.

For Sue to know who she is and to learn how to live without her partner, she must continue to be open to discovering the different losses that have occurred. Naming them opens her eyes to the fullness of their relationship and the multiple ways that their shared life had defined who they each were. (This will also become a valuable resource for joy when she enters the dimension of gratitude.)

Naming the losses of our lives isn't simply the work of those who have involuntarily lost something. It happens with any significant loss, even if it is the natural consequence of achieving what you have desired.

Helen had been in school most of her life. She had been a good student in high school and had scholarships to an Ivy League university. She did very well in philosophy and religion and decided to get her masters in theology. She loved the study of theology so much, she decided to get her PhD and become a professor.

When she finally achieved her goal and received her diploma, Helen went into a depression. She was not prepared for the losses she encountered. She knew she would miss the students she had been in school with. They talked about that. But what she didn't realize was that she was losing much more. As she began to talk about it and live the emptiness, she discovered she had lost a sense of security. She knew how to be a student—she had been perfecting that skill for twenty years. Now she had to be a teacher. And while she had seen others do it, she didn't have the confidence she had known as a student.

Furthermore, as a student, others had set the standards and rules. Others had defined success for her. Others had given her direction on how to carry out her passion. But as a teacher, she had to direct herself. She lost the security of being able to satisfy others even as she opened up to discovering what she thought was important to be doing.

As she kept naming what this PhD had cost her, Helen discovered she no longer had her dream to drive her. For twenty years she had been driven by getting the next degree. Her dream to get a PhD was a powerful motivator. She felt flat and without direction without the dream to energize her. She had doubts about whether theology was really that interesting after all.

It is important for Helen to continue exploring the different levels of loss so that she can clarify the truth about her future. She clearly loved philosophy and theology, but she had never had the privilege of loving it apart from the goal of achieving the degree. She must understand that a powerful part of her life's experience to this point was a love of theology combined with a goal. When she knows this, she can then begin to move on toward living life in the absence of that particular goal. She can move toward freedom to name other goals that might motivate her in the future. She can discover delight in the drive to help students learn the subjects that excite her or to fulfill a new dream of publishing her ideas for others to explore.

This process of grieving loss is very similar to the process of taking a spiritual pilgrimage. Those who take a pilgrimage have a profound longing for some experience of the holy that can

> *One of the things that is so important in this pilgrimage is to name that which you must give up to take it.*

happen when they reach the holy city or shrine. That longing is so powerful it causes them to leave home to achieve it. One of the things that is so important in this pilgrimage is to name that which you must give up to take it. To leave home for a long period of time means you will lose the experience of those you love who stay behind. Changing your life to go on the road means you will cause greater stress on the family and the friends you leave, for someone must cover your responsibilities.

Moreover, when you return, they will lose you the way you were. You will be a new person, shaped in new ways by the experiences you have had. Only as you are able to name the losses you will experience, and as you guard against allowing those losses to control your actions, will you have the courage to leave home. To grieve and grow requires noticing and naming the lived experiences of multiple losses.

Good Companions

As you journey through this early part of the process of grieving loss and growing spiritually, it is advisable to find good companions to travel with you. A fitting person for this part of the discovery is someone who is good at asking questions. It is someone who can help you name the various dimensions of the loss you are experiencing.

Some people are eager for you to see the benefits of the loss. They will constantly remind you of what you have gained. If you have had a miscarriage, they will be eager for you to know you can always try again. These folks are not helpful. At this point in the process, it is good to have people who will just let you tell your story over and over, trusting that if it is important to you, it is important to them. You need someone who trusts you are smart enough to see the obvious but that it takes some patience to see the more subtle and meaningful parts of this loss. Good companions are those people who don't need you to be the way you were. These are the individuals who can allow you to be just the way you are.

Good friends are people who listen well. When we are in the midst of the collapse of a world as we have known it, we need to speak about it. No one can talk us out of our loss or pain. We must talk ourselves out of our pain, our guilt, and our fear and talk ourselves into the new life that is growing in us.

Good listeners create an empty space—an empty container—which can receive the spoken losses as they pour forth, remember them, and hold them for you so that when you are able, you can come back to them and sort through them. By listening and remembering your stories, good companions can mirror them back to you when you are able to hear them and claim them. These insights will help you discover why you continue to feel sadness and help you discover the surprising richness of your lost relationships.

Any kind of growth requires giving up one thing for something else. The ability to develop clarity about the different things you have to give up will help free you to move toward the new life, the new sense of self you desire. Naming the losses in the presence of good companions who accept you as you are is a valuable part of this growing process.

Feeling Pain

To learn to live again also requires that we *experience the pain of the loss*. This part of the process interacts closely with naming the loss. The feeling of the pain speaks of what we have lost. Naming those losses helps clarify the feelings. And feeling the pain helps you name more of what is lost.

Following the initial numbing shock of disbelief in the immediate experience of loss, pain presses itself into our soul and body. It is sometimes more than we think we can bear. We seek ways to anesthetize ourselves. It hurts too much to allow that gaping hole in our gut to bleed unstaunched. We want to do anything else but feel that pain. We want to fill the empty cut within with something—alcohol, drugs, sex, sleep, work, easy love, TV. We are vulnerable to anyone who will offer us a moment's respite from that unspeakable canyon within our soul.

But feeling pain is important. It first of all reminds us that we are alive. Following the cutting off of someone or something that matters deeply, our body protects us by numbing us. I remember breaking my leg as I slipped on the ice. I got up and walked two blocks home, thinking it didn't hurt very badly. But then after sitting for an hour and making arrangements to go to the emergency room, it hurt so much I could not move.

The body helps us deal with the shock of pain with initial anesthetic. The body does this for broken hearts as well. We receive help so the reality of the loss can soak in. We can't stand the truth all at once.

Eventually though, we begin to feel again. And the pain reminds us we are still alive. It will come and go, visiting us at times we least expect it. When the pain of sadness and loneliness are felt, know that this is a sign you are growing stronger. When we are not strong, the body numbs us and we don't feel. But when we feel the pain, we are gaining strength. Tears are not a sign of weakness but a sign of strength. Pain reminds us that something important has happened. It reminds us that to be human is to feel. It is only when we can feel the deep sadness of the loss that we can ever hope to feel the deep joy of new life. Feeling is central to the ability to experience the fullness of life as it is being lived.

Feeling the pain also teaches us truth. When we have had a significant loss, it is tempting to live in denial. It is easy to pretend the loss has not really

> *Following the cutting off of someone or something that matters deeply, our body protects us by numbing us.*

happened. Frank lost his wife to cancer. After forty years of living in the same house together, he was devastated. Many mornings he would get up and imagine he could smell the coffee as she had begun to brew it. For a moment he would begin to speak to her as if she were in the other room. Our hearts protect us from the full truth of the loss until we can absorb it bit by bit. The feeling of the pain of the loss teaches us the truth that the loss is real.

And truth is important for the ability to move toward the new life which is waiting for us. Until we know that the past is truly gone, we might imagine that we can live that life over again. Some people get married soon after the death of a partner. Unless they have felt the pain of the truth of the loss, they might try to replicate the life they had. The temptation is that the new partner will be a replacement partner. Sometimes the new partner is an old friend of the one who has died. The heart longs for the familiar and will try to re-create it any way possible. They want the new person in their life to make it as comfortable as the old person did. This, of course, is impossible, and disappointment will be a major problem in the new relationship unless they are certain, deep in their bones, that the person they once loved is not and will never again be present to offer their love.

Living with the painful truth of absence for a significant period of time is important. This gives the grieving person time to allow pain to produce more awareness of all the things that have been lost and to name them. Just as pain in the body is a sign that something needs attention, so pain in the heart is a sign that something still exists that we need to be mindful of.

Feeling the pain is also important for helping the body release the toxins created by suffering. Tears can be a healing release of the whole system when they are allowed to flow.

I am a white male whose culture taught me to not cry. Crying was a sign of weakness, and I was not supposed to be weak. When my first wife died, however, I was initially overcome with tears. They would not stop. As the demands of work and life took over, I gave up the tears. But the pain did not give up on me.

I was still experiencing many layers of loss, but I could not cry. I would just get surly and angry. I would be hard to live with. I got blue and depressed—but I did not cry. Then I saw the movie *Shadowlands* about the short life and love of C. S. Lewis and his wife, Joy. Joy died of cancer after a brief but powerful relationship. That movie helped me release the tears and express my sadness. The pain was eased as I was free to feel it and express it. For several years after that, when I began to ignore my sadness and pain, I watched the movie and found release in my soul and body.

Tears are an important way for us to find release from the pain of our loss. There are those who advise us that we should give up our pain and get on with our life. They believe the task of grieving is just deciding that you are over it. My experience suggests pain and sadness are not something we can choose to lose. Pain has to give up on us. Tears are a way of helping us rinse out our souls so that the sadness releases its grip on us.

It is also important to feel the pain of loss so as to activate the imagination for our new life. If we don't deeply feel our loss, our imagination will be reluctant to envision new ways of being. Helen, our PhD friend, had to feel the pain of the loss of her dream so that an empty space could be

> *Pain is present. And to attend to it is to be in the here and now.*

created for new dreams. As the old goals fade into the familiarity of normal, the new and interesting goals have the freedom to visit via the imagination.

Feeling pain is also important for learning to live anew because pain helps us notice the present. Much of our time is spent worrying and planning for the future or worrying and agonizing over the past. We spend much of our energy trying to fill the empty unknown of the future or to rethink the mistakes we might have made in the past. Pain is present. And to attend to it is to be in the here and now.

If we are going to live a new life, if we are going to notice and embrace a life that is coming to us in the future, we have to have the ability to be alive and attentive to the present. Pain has the power to cause us to focus on ourselves. Paying attention to ourselves is an important part of the process to becoming the new person we hope to be.

There is one other reason to feel the pain. To feel the pain of a love lost is a sign that we have indeed loved. We seldom feel unquenchable agony when we lose something we don't love. It is only the capacity to love that makes it possible to feel such deep emotional and spiritual pain. When we do not avoid the pain but feel it, we are reminded that love is real and that we have a capacity to love—that is, to live.

Now there is a danger in feeling pain. We can become addicted to it. That is, since it makes us feel that we are alive, it is sometimes hard to let go of. By remembering the loss over and over, we feel the pain, the love, and the life, over and over. But sometimes the pain becomes a substitute for loving and living in the future. Sometimes it takes on a life of its own.

Many of our friends and family will want to help us ease the pain. And it is understandable. It is hard for any of us to be around deep pain as it infects people we love. It is natural for us to want to fix them if we are able. This impulse to help ease the pain often tempts us to say things which are not helpful.

"You'll be fine."

"I know how you feel."

"It's time to get on with your life."

Each of these statements may be true, but they are seldom helpful when we are overwhelmed with pain.

What is helpful in the experiencing of the pain is having persons who can walk with us in it. It is being around people who do not need us to be feeling well all the time. It is being with a counselor or confidant or friend who does not like to see us in pain but who does not need to hurry us through it so they might feel better. It is being with people who can be present to the pain and help us see what it is that we might learn from it. People who know we are strong and that, given enough time and feeling, we will grow through the experience are invaluable companions for this journey.

Just as losing results in pain, so spiritual growth is painful as well. For us to grow spiritually, there are some things with which we must part so there is room for new things to come into our life. Our spirit is shaped by that which we love. What we love requires our

> *For us to grow spiritually, there are some things with which we must part so there is room for new things to come into our life.*

time and attention. When we attend to one thing, we don't have as much time for other things. The pain of that loss must be experienced.

Jeff and Alice had been married for three years. They decided it was time to have a family. Alice got pregnant, and excitement built. The presence of a new person in the family expanded their world beyond their imagination. The birthing experience was one of the most powerful experiences of their lives. Participating in the creative energy of the universe overwhelmed them with awe. The moment of birth bonded them in ways nothing else had.

But as their spirits expanded in awe, their pain over the fate of little babies in the refugee camps of the world dug deep in their souls. Their concern grew and they began to raise money to provide services for those babies. As they grew in their love for their child and other children, however, their time to spend traveling to see siblings and friends diminished. Their work for babies created a dull discomfort that was related to what they were losing. They felt that discomfort, got in touch with it, and named it. While that alone didn't heal the hurt, it at least enabled them to give themselves to their new passion wholeheartedly and not think there was something wrong with it.

Feeling pain is powerful and important for our growing toward a new life when something has changed in our life.

Good Companions

One of the characteristics of a good companion in this dimension of living loss is a person who is not afraid of feeling their own pain. When we are with a person we care about who is hurting deeply, it makes us hurt as well. If we are able to endure our own pain that gets stirred up when sharing it with others, we can be present with people when they hurt.

It is also good to be with a person who does not need to fix you. When we are feeling pain and knowing the life force through that feeling, we don't need someone to get us out of that feeling. As painful as it might be, it is something that helps us know we were loved and cared for. We don't want to lose that feeling too quickly, because we will feel more alone when it goes away. No one can save us from our pain. They might distract us for a while (and that can be a gift), but our pain is our own business.

A good companion for you while you are feeling pain is also someone who can just be quiet and hold your hand. Pain is selfish, and when we feel it deeply, we need someone who can let us be where we are and not expect us to give of ourselves for their well-being.

It is helpful to have friends who are simply present, because when we are numb, we often feel disconnected from the strength of the community we have known. The steadfast presence of someone who just shows up from time to time reminds us that we still belong, even if we don't feel like it. It reminds us we are remembered, even if we don't want to remember.

Often the best friends in this time are old ones—people who know you well enough and are tender enough to gently help you come out of yourself from time to time. Old friends know deeply your pain because they have shared your life. They know what the loss means to you. Because they have lived with you, their presence reminds you of the presence that has been lost.

This kind of presence takes a really good friend. It takes a person who trusts that we will eventually "come in out of the rain" and assures us by their confidence that they will be there when we are able to give of ourselves again.

Anger

A third dimension of the experience of loss and growth is the emotion of anger. Anger is, among other things, the response the body feels when it senses a threat. When we lose someone or something that has helped us know a significant portion of who we are, we feel threatened.

When Tom retired, he was surprised by how much anger and rage he felt. He had been looking forward to his retirement as a time to do all the things he had not had time for. But a few weeks after he stopped going to work, he felt angry and disquieted.

What happened is that Tom had spent forty years of his life as a science teacher and coach at the local high school. And when that came to an end, his self-understanding was threatened. He did not realize how much his sense of worth was tied up in the portion of his identity he defined by teaching and coaching.

One way to imagine this and the impact of a loss is with overlapping circles (see Illustration 1). Tom is the larger circle in the middle of the picture. One circle is his role as Malinda's father. Another circle is as Jack's father. Another circle is as Carolyn's husband. Another circle represents his shared life with his father. Another, his life with his mother. Another, his life as a teacher.

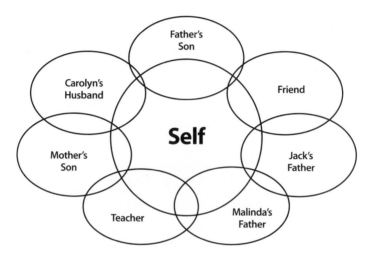

Illustration 1: Sense of Self

When Tom retired, a large chunk of his self-understanding was torn away (see Illustration 2)—it wasn't simply his self-understanding as a teacher. That self-understanding impacted the way he related to the other people in his life. Tom's sense of confidence in his own identity was confused. His identity was threatened.

Confusion about our identity often feels like a threat. Anger is the body's production of adrenaline, which enables the animal in us to fight or flee that which threatens us. It is raw energy that needs to go somewhere. Anger is an honest emotion that must be accepted and addressed or it will go underground in the soul and eat away at our life and vitality.

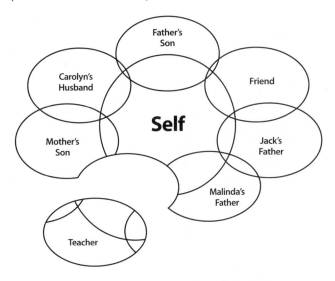

Illustration 2: Identity Confusion

The focus of our anger may vary. Sometimes it is channeled outward. When Barbara and Jim lost their six-month-old baby to SID, among other things they felt amid the devastation were rage and anger. They were angry at the medical community for not being able to prevent such a tragedy. They were angry with other people whose children were still alive. They were angry at the world for not slowing down and taking into account their pain. They were angry with God for allowing such a sweet child to simply die. They were angry at the faith community for their powerlessness in the face of such loss.

Sometimes when we lose our innocence, we get angry at the world as well. Several years ago I was on a trip to Cambodia. It is one of the poorest countries in the world, having suffered the massive genocide of Pol Pot. I was overwhelmed by the stories of death and destruction. I was moved to tears by little children who did not have food.

When I returned to the wealth of my own country, I was angry. I was angry at advertisers for manipulating our greed. I was angry at our government for not caring enough for the rest of the world. I was angry at multinational corporations who only served their own best interests and cared nothing for the foreign workers who made their success possible. When my eyes were opened to the reality of the world I had only seen on television, my own understanding of myself and my nation as good and caring was challenged. I was angry at the world over my loss of innocence.

Anger at loss might also be focused inward. Mike was close to his mother. He had never really left home even though he was forty-two years old. He and his mother got along well except for the times she challenged him about getting a place of his own.

One night Mike's mother had a heart attack. Mike was out with friends. When he came home, he found her on the couch, dead.

Mike experienced both sadness and fear. But he was also angry. He was angry because he was not there when she needed him. He was angry at his mother. But he was angrier at himself, for he felt he had brought on the attack by not getting a place of his own. Mike channeled his anger toward himself. He became depressed and was hospitalized.

To be angry is a natural response to loss. Getting down on

ourselves because we're angry, however, does no good. Feeling it, naming
it, and expressing it in ways that don't
abuse ourselves or others helps us release anger.

> *Anger is energy that*
> *can help us build a*
> *new identity.*

To know and feel our anger can
help us focus and use that anger in constructive ways. Anger is energy that can help us build a new identity. Focusing our anger on
what we can do to live a new life gets us away from being a victim
and the desire for someone else to save us from our fears. We can
explore what makes us feel strong and what helps us form a new
identity not dependent upon what is lost.

It is worth noting that anger is not the only emotion to be
mindful of when our identity is threatened. Fear can feed our
anger. Terror and fear are often present when we have had a
significant loss. Because we are unclear about ourselves, we are
unclear about what we are capable of. And if we don't know
what our capacities are, we are fearful that we won't have what
is needed to make it in life.

Andrea was terrified. She had trusted Bill to be faithful to
his word. She had believed their marriage was solid. When Bill
told her he had a brief affair, Andrea was furious. Her anger
was fed not only by her sense of betrayal, but because of the
loss of trust. She didn't know what to trust any more. She had
somehow believed that the future would look something like
the past and she would be sharing life with Bill. But now she
didn't know. She was afraid the home and the life she had built

with Bill would crumble. She was afraid she could not support herself and her children. She was afraid her children would grow up in a home unlike the home she had always dreamed of. Her fear intensified her anger and made it difficult for her to imagine a way to build a future.

When our identity is threatened we may also experience anxiety. Anxiety comes from a word which means "to choke." When we feel frightened and unclear about who we are, we can become anxious. But when our inner strength grows, and we discover we don't need what has been lost to be someone we like and feel good about, we become less anxious. When our anxiety is lessened, we are able to see more options for our future and thus are likely to make better decisions.

I experienced that when I became a professor. Even though I had taught most of my life as a pastor, my image of what a professor was differed from my image of a teaching pastor. Therefore I was deeply anxious the first couple of years I taught in the seminary. I didn't know what my capacities were. I had unrealistic expectations and had to discover what "realistic" might be. I even had troubling dreams at night, adding to my difficulty in dealing with my fear.

As we struggle to grow and change and deal with the losses that accompany those changes, it is very important to allow ourselves to feel the anger that rises up. It is important to express it in ways that are consistent with the truth of what is causing it. That means we should not strike out at our children when we are feeling threatened by a possible job loss.

Being in touch with our anger and fear and anxiety is a very important part of growing spiritually. To grow spiritually is to center our lives in that which can sustain us in the midst of the changing world around us. Spiritual strength is the ability to stay on course even when the winds of threat and fear would knock us off. If we are in touch with our fears and our anger, then we are more aware of what we are putting our trust in. To trust our souls to those things that can be taken from us is to be vulnerable to manipulation by the powers that would control us. But to trust in the energy of life that creates and re-creates us, ever calling us into a new world, is to be defined by that which has eternal qualities.

When we are processing loss or growing spiritually, we will feel anger. Let this be and let it teach us. Live the anger and fear and anxiety. It isn't easy. But know it is normal. There is nothing wrong with you. It is a dimension of the experience of learning to live again.

Good Companions

A good companion through this experience of growth and grief is one who is not afraid of passion and fire. Anger is scary. It is full of energy and chaos. It often feels like you are spinning out of control. A good companion is one who is not blown over by powerful emotions.

Someone who doesn't take attacks personally is helpful. She knows there is nothing that anyone can do to fill all your needs for security and safety. She knows you may strike out against her but it really isn't about her. She knows you are just scared and don't know who else to scream at.

A good friend is also one who can help you name what you are afraid of. You may not even know what frightens you. When Deborah and I were on our honeymoon in St. John, we went snorkeling in the Caribbean. As we floated around looking at the underwater life, I kept breathing in water in my mask. It was frustrating. It spoiled the beauty and the fun. Finally Deborah asked me, "Are you afraid?"

I immediately replied, "No, I'm not afraid. What would I be afraid of? I know how to swim."

But as I kept trying to relax and breathe easily, I realized that I was afraid. I had not spent much time in the ocean. I sheepishly confessed to Deborah and she said, "Let me hold your hand."

And so I did. And with just a few moments of her calming presence, I was released from my fear and could move away from her hand and snorkel on my own.

Good companions are ones who can feel and help you name your passions, your fears, and then be present to ease the fears till you can swim on your own.

It is also good to have musical companions. Poetry and music are ways of expressing that which is too deep for expression. Passionate music and artistic expression that articulates anger and fear, terror and agony can be very helpful during our angry times. We need people around us who can help us find ways to express these deep physical emotions so we can share our feelings.

The visual arts also provide healing perspectives. I have a friend who has photographs of tornadoes as his computer screen saver. He says they remind him of the turmoil of his soul and its potentially destructive power. Paintings and photographs that open us to our own fear and chaos help us stay in touch with who we are and what we are experiencing.

It is also beneficial to have people around us who can hear the self-doubt that drives much of our anger. It is shattering to realize you don't have the power to keep loss from happening and that many times there is no power to restore it. We need individuals who can hold on to our confidence for us even when we doubt everything about ourselves.

Remembering

A fourth part of the growing-through-grieving process is *remembering*. To learn to live again is to spend time remembering what has been lost. We have all retold our story of loss over and over. Sometimes we think we must be boring other people because we can't seem to stop telling how he died. We tell anyone who will listen—stranger or friend—as we try to come to terms with the absence of someone important to us.

The reason this is such a continuous process is that significant losses are a loss to the whole self. They affect the mind, heart, body, and soul. The mind, for example, becomes disoriented. We orient ourselves in relationship to significant people and things. Whether or not we know it, the space we live in becomes an orienting factor. When someone loses their home to flood or fire, their mind becomes disoriented. It is hard to get a sense of comfort and space. When we are not in familiar spaces, our mind

> *Loss is a physical experience.*
> *The body has ways of knowing that seem to ignore the mind and heart.*

must work overtime to know where we are and therefore where we might be going. Part of the reason we keep talking about the house and the way it used to be is to help us reorganize our mind.

Loss has a debilitating effect on the heart as well. The heart is where the affective part of our relationships is carried. It is the part of us that bonds to the other. When we are bonded, we are a part of their life and they are a part of ours. When we lose a loved one, the heart is stripped of some of its way of knowing itself. To remember, to "re-member" the other person, is the heart's way of reorganizing the shattered and scattered pieces of our life.

To lose someone significant is a loss to the body as well. Loss is a physical experience. The body has ways of knowing that seem to ignore the mind and heart. In the early years after my first wife died, I found myself getting distressed in the springtime. My body would become restless and unsettled. It took a couple of years to realize that my body was remembering the death long before my mind or heart remembered. In some way, deep within the bone marrow, the body has ways of holding the pain of loss that does not require the heart or mind to participate. When we spend time telling the story of the loss, we are trying to get the body to come to terms with the loss.

Loss reaches deep in the soul too. When our child dies, our

soul is stripped of much of the comfort and security it had constructed for itself. The soul may have had a fundamental trust of the universe or God, but when a child is taken from us, the soul must fundamentally reorient itself. The world will never be as friendly as it was before. Underlying the hope for a beneficent world is the truth that lurking at the edges of our fragile hope is the threat of death and chaos. To remember, to tell the story over and over, is the soul's way of trying to re-understand and know itself in relation to the forces that hold life and threaten life.

It could be said that remembering is the way we come to "full-body" knowing. When we tell of the one we have lost, we are integrating our body, mind, heart, and soul so that all of who we are fully experiences the truth of the loss.

It is important to tell the story frequently because your partner in memory is not there with you. When people who remember with you are not around, you lose a sense of history. Shared history is important for a sense of continuity and intimacy. When you are no longer with a person who shares your history, remembering helps keep that intimacy alive. The memories will never re-create the presence, but memories will still provide foundations on which to build your future.

Remembering, however, is more than the integrative process. It is a way of slowing down and finding rest in the familiar. Adapting to change and processing the loss that accompanies it is physically, emotionally, spiritually, and intellectually exhausting. To spend time re-membering the reality that has been lost is a way of resting and allowing your energy to be replenished.

It is also a way of creating a memorial. Humans create memorials to powerful experiences of passion. Memorials must represent the magnitude of the experience. New York struggles to come up with the right memorial to represent the evil, terror, heroism, and agony of the attack on the twin towers on 9/11. We need something to remind us of its size and of the particular losses of each soul in the rubble. To do this, we have to go over the plans many times to find something (inadequate and impotent as it might be) that represents the fullness of the experience.

And we must remember our loss long enough that it becomes human. Many times when we lose someone in divorce, the offended party makes a demon out of the one who violated the marriage. If we lose someone to death, we may make a saint out of the one who died. Neither reality is finally true. Unless we remember long enough to see that those who are lost were human with all the mixture of good and bad that is present in any of us, our future will be distorted. If the one who left in a divorce remains only dark and evil in the memory of the one left, she might be inclined to never love again or to go on a passionate search for the perfect man. If we lose a lover to death and do not remember long enough that the truth about her humanity comes into focus, we may never be able to love another for who they are—complaining because they do not live up to the saint we once loved. This dimension of the growing-through-grieving process is fundamental to the discovery of life through loss.

Another dimension closely tied to remembering is forgiveness. We will see later that forgiveness is what humans offer each other.

Forgiveness requires some sense of power, and if we see those we have lost as possessing divine power, it will be very difficult for us to learn to move beyond their power into our own power. Remembering the whole of what is lost is critical.

The creating of a memorial in the mind and heart is also important as a way of taking control of your life again. A memorial is a pocket-sized collection of memories that we can take with us, look at and remember when we want to, and then put away. Jane lost her child to a rare illness. When the loss first occurred, little Melody was everywhere Jane looked. Every piece of clothing had her smell. Every room in the house was filled with her presence. Every song she heard and every child she saw reminded her of Melody, and the cutting pain in her heart bled again and again. Jane obsessed about Melody. She talked to whoever would listen.

One day Jane was talking to a friend and found out there was a little boy with the same disease who could not afford treatment. This created such pain in Jane that she decided to do something about it. She started a fund to help little Bobby get treatment. Out of that fund grew a memorial fund for little children who needed help getting treatment. Jane's energy and Melody's spirit, which were ever present everywhere, coalesced into a particular focus. Jane could now focus her memory so that it wasn't in every nook and cranny in the house and in the community.

Every time she saw a sick child, she remembered Melody's death, and unbearable pain rose from deep within her and almost overwhelmed her. But she endured that pain, allowed it

> *The work of remembering is downsizing the reality so it can be carried within us into the future.*

to exist, and moved with it to ease the pain of other children and parents. Every child she met and helped added another thread to the fabric of the memorial she was creating to honor her little girl.

Sometimes such a memorial helps the senselessness of tragedy to have some sense. It will never make sense in terms of the heart, but at least the absurdity of the death has the chance of having some meaning. When you have suffered a significant loss and other people can benefit from your experience, there is at least some hope. By focusing the memory and the energy on the future, the life of the past becomes power for growing your world. As a result of this memorial, Jane has been able to expand her world, and her heart has been touched by dozens of parents and children whom she would have never known.

The memorial-making we do shrinks the pervasive absence of the one we have lost. In its place, fresh space is created for new people, new relationships, and new life.

The danger of remembering is getting stuck. It is hard to know when we have remembered long enough. No one can tell us when to get over it. The work of remembering is downsizing the reality so it can be carried within us into the future. We must create a memorial inside our souls so the life of love that was known still remains alive in us, but doesn't control our loving in the future.

The communities of faith, of which many are a part, know this act of remembering is central to the new life they invite others to experience. The Jewish community is constantly reminded to remember the liberating power of God to bring people from slavery to freedom. The Christian community is constantly called to remember the life and death and resurrection of Jesus. Both are called to remember in hopes of full liberation and healing—effects closely related to God's future hope for humanity.

To remember is a critical part of learning to live in the future amid profound loss. Keep remembering. Don't let others discourage your memories. Let the memories play over your heart and mind, bathing you in the pain and pleasure they bring.

Good Companions

Helpful companions are people who have time. The process of remembering all the consequences of a loss requires slow time. It requires "porch swing" time. It needs the presence of people whose ease with just sitting and chatting is not obsessed with getting things done.

A good friend is one with whom you can rest and be at ease. Some people seem to be ill at ease when you spend time telling your story over and over. They cut you off by saying, "You told me that before." It may be that this friend should be one who has a bad memory so that each time you tell the story, they hear it afresh.

Good companions are also ones who can help us create a memorial to what is lost. Ann's six year old daughter Grace died suddenly of a virulent form of strep. When Grace's sixth birthday came around, there was just an empty space where the parties of celebration had been. Some of Ann's cousins gathered with her and took her to a tattoo parlor—not a place Ann frequented. After looking at every kind of picture and finding nothing appropriate, Ann's cousin drew a couple of small bells ringing. (Grace's self-proclaimed nickname was "Gracie Belle.") The tattoo artist's needle buzzed, and now whenever Ann looks down at the inside of her ankle, she sees pink bells ringing—a constant memorial to her little girl. Good companions go with us when we need to find ways to remember.

Helpful companions for this dimension of the growing process are individuals who do not have some preconceived notion of what moving on for you would look like. They need to be open to whatever you are remembering, not wondering when you are going to move to a place where you don't need to remember so much. They know that remembering is a way of resting in familiar places and that this exhausting process requires frequent resting places.

5 Guilt

A fifth dimension of growing through change and grieving the loss of that which has been significant is the *experience of guilt*. This may surprise people, especially if you are not particularly religious. Some people believe guilt is the creation of religious people who want to control others. And indeed, it has been exploited by religion to keep people under control.

The fact is, in spite of what we might want to think, guilt is real. To be in community, to live within human circles of care, means people take responsibility for living with each other. When we take responsibility for relationships, we give to and receive from each other. If I am part of a family, I have some negotiated responsibility within that family structure. I may be responsible for making some money to support the family. I may be responsible for contributing to the safety of the children. I may be responsible for helping out with the dishes or taking out the garbage. Responsibility is inherent within any community that has stability and purpose.

That being said, guilt is a real dimension of responsible communities. Guilt is the term used when someone does not fulfill their task. Guilt is the term used when we do not give what we have claimed we will give. Therefore, whenever there is a significant loss, we begin to raise questions about what we should or should not have done.

I have been with many people as they have grieved the loss of a marriage. I know of no one who goes into marriage without the expectation that it will last. Most people I know believe the decisions they make in the relationship will contribute to its well-being and its longevity. Most people begin their marriage trying to live in a way that contributes to the happiness of the two people in the marriage.

As the marriage progresses, some issues arise that become difficult to process. Frequently there are arguments and fights. Two people who have independent thoughts will disagree. During the arguments or fights, each will be hurt. Each will wound the other—intentionally or unintentionally. Most of the painful disagreements include not only the sharing of different ideas but the challenge of ideas that represent what we believe about ourselves. When these arguments cut into our feelings about the character of the other, the pain is deep and the hurt is real. If this goes on long enough, some marriages hit the wall and someone decides to leave the marriage.

Most people who are honest about their divorces will say

there was plenty in the relationship that contributed to the demise of the marriage. And most people would say there was enough responsibility to go around. After the painful departure when each person is trying to defend themselves against the accusations of the other, each can think of things that happened during the marriage they might have done differently. Frequently they feel guilty about not having done those things that would have saved the marriage.

Now this kind of guilt isn't simply related to two adults in a relationship. It is sometimes visited on those who believe they had power to make a difference but didn't. Michael was thirteen when his parents divorced. His own turmoil as an early adolescent was combined with the tension in the marriage between his parents. When they finally separated, Michael carried a lot of guilt. He felt like his angry outbursts and his resistance to his parents' requests were responsible for his parents splitting up.

Guilt isn't just limited to relationships for which we have responsibility and power to act. Guilt also seems to be present even when there was nothing we could do. Gary is weighted with a guilt he can hardly stand. His daughter had just turned sixteen and had her license. She wanted to borrow the family car and visit a friend. Gary agreed and gave her the keys. Just a mile from their home, his daughter was struck broadside by a car that ran a red light. His daughter was killed.

Mixed in with all the pain and aching agony of losing his daughter was a sense of guilt. This would not have happened had he just said no. Maybe he had not been a good enough teacher and

63

taught his daughter about defensive driving. If he had just bought the new car he had been putting off, the side airbags would have saved her life. Guilt rides the vehicles of "what if" and "if only," driving us to near insanity. It is not enough to tell Gary he is not responsible. He feels responsible, and guilt will be his constant companion.

> *It is important to sort out what we are really responsible for and what we have no power to control.*

Many believe that this kind of guilt is closer to a primal shame. Some therapists believe that when an infant is born, she has a sense that she is the center of the universe. She believes she has power to make people around her do what she needs done. But early on there is a growing sense that she can't make things happen that affect her. She comes to know within her soul that she does not have power to control her world. She feels inadequate. Some would say this sense of inadequacy produces shame. We feel we are not worthy because we don't have the power to make things happen that would be good for us.

This is the reason that one must spend time dealing with this in the grieving process. It is important to sort out what we are really responsible for and what we have no power to control. If we can get an honest assessment of our responsibility and what real power we have to change things, then we can open ourselves to forgiveness. We can be open to knowing that we made certain mistakes but not carry around the burden of believing we could have changed everything.

Processing is important even if you can't ever think your way out of it. It is always important to sort out what power you actually have. Sometimes our sense of guilt is related to our belief that we have godly power. Molly's husband died. Molly was a religious woman and she went to church regularly. When Molly's husband got sick with cancer, Molly prayed for his healing. She was in a community who prayed as well. Earnest petitions were sent up to God on behalf of her husband. But he did not survive.

One part of Molly's mind knew she could not have saved her husband. But another part would not give up on the idea that she had not prayed hard enough. And she somehow believed her prayers were not answered because she was not good enough. Had she been a better person, God would have answered her prayer. Guilt rested squarely inside Molly's soul.

Understanding guilt and processing what our responsibility and our power actually is helps us move beyond the painful losses of our lives. Exploring our feelings will help us give up our need and desire to be divine. It will help us realize we are human and that all we can give is what we have. Discovering our responsibility for a broken relationship is an important part of opening up to forgiveness.

Naming our limits and accepting our humanity also opens us up to the delightful human future beyond our pain. When we discover our limits, we are not tempted to over function in the future. If we believe we have omnipotent power, we will always worry we are not doing enough to make things work out better. We will be tempted to believe everything is about us and that we must do

> *Discovering our responsibility for a broken relationship is an important part of opening up to forgiveness.*

everything right to ensure nothing goes wrong. But if we know we can only influence certain things and that there are many things out of our control, then we can do well with what is our responsibility and not carry around unreal expectations for ourselves. Many people miss the sheer delight of living because they take on more responsibility than is theirs to take.

When we are realistic about our responsibility, then we can be realistic about our mistakes. We can work on things that can be corrected. In the PBS documentary *What I Want My Words to Do to You*, Eve Ensler spends several months working with inmates in a maximum security prison for women. She guides them in a writing workshop that helps the women sort out what about their situation was the result of their choices and where they were victimized. In working this out, they begin to realize that they are more than the mistakes they have made. Ensler tells the prison population that society creates prisons as monuments to the mistakes these women made. Before she worked with these women she saw them as mistakes. They had become their mistakes. But after she worked with them, she saw them as women who had made mistakes.

This is the growing that can occur when we admit we feel guilty when there is a loss. If we stay with our feelings and explore the truth about our responsibilities and our limits, we cannot become a mistake, but we can see ourselves as persons who make mistakes and who are therefore capable of forgiveness, which frees us from the power of those mistakes so we can come alive in a new future.

Good Companions

People who walk well with us as we experience guilt are people who know guilt in their own lives. They are people who know they have made mistakes and understand that you feel you have made them too. You do not need someone to talk you out of your feelings. They can't do it. It is just irritating. You need someone to affirm your feelings of guilt.

You also need individuals around who have experienced grace. We all have been loved when we don't deserve it. And when we are feeling pain and not liking ourselves, we need people around who know what it is like to have received love when they didn't feel worthy of it. This kind of person is one who stays present and is not pushed away by your "bitchiness" or your selfishness. They love you even when you don't know yourself as lovable.

And, it is good if this person can ask thoughtful questions. It is always helpful to sort through what you have responsibility for and what is beyond your capacity. It is not easy to admit we don't have the power to make things right or to bring back someone who has gone, but by helping us think about it over and over, we eventually come to accept what is ours and what is not ours.

If you are a religious person, it is helpful to walk a while with a person of faith who can assure you that your community trusts in forgiveness. Priests, pastors, and rabbis have the responsibility to tell the stories of faith or the doctrine of the church or synagogue that reflects the mercy of God for creatures. Some will help you find ways to open yourself to that forgiving mercy by offering activities which offset the mistake you might have made. Others will assure you that the community of which you are a part and the God you worship loves you and will stay with you even if you feel guilty.

If you are a person of faith, it is also good to reread stories of your ancestors where mercy and grace were made evident. Jews, Muslims, and Christians all share common stories of God's mercy. An early story of Cain and Abel reveals a God whose mercy extends to one who has killed his brother. While there is some penalty for the crime, there is also an opportunity to live life, to create family, and to have a future. This and many other stories told within the faith community help us realize that guilt is real and that forgiveness is possible. Knowing this opens us to receiving forgiving grace for our future.

6 *Forgiving*

The way to new life, or the way to living without the presence of someone or something that has been significant, requires that a person live through several dimensions of life.

- When someone wishes to grow and move beyond where they are, it is very important to *name the losses* that have happened or that will happen when they move away.

- *Feeling the pain* of the loss helps you know more deeply the truth of the loss.

- *Getting in touch with anger* that resides in the loss helps you discover energy for new life.

- *Remembering what is lost* helps free us from a free-floating memory and focuses that memory so we can move into the future.

- *Identifying the guilt* we feel because of what we did or did not do to contribute to the loss, or the guilt we feel over not having power to stave off the loss, helps us discover the limits of our own humanness.

When we have experienced these things, sometimes we are visited with the gift of *a forgiving spirit*. When we have struggled and identified the experiences of our humanity and the humanity of others, we may find ourselves being more gracious toward ourselves or others in our lives. A forgiving spirit is a gift that comes to us when we are no longer dependent on what we have lost for our sense of well-being.

It is important to realize that forgiveness is not freedom from the memory of the past. We don't forgive and forget. The past is an important part of who we are. The pain is central to our new self-understanding. Remembering the pain protects us from getting into situations that are dangerous for us.

Sally was taught that forgiveness and forgetfulness was a virtue to be cherished. She was in a relationship with a man who abused her. Her marriage to this man bound her not only to him as he cherished her but also as he beat her. She believed that her faith required that she forgive him. For her, this included forgetting the abuse for which she forgave him. Because she bound forgiveness with forgetting, she continued to expose herself to a life that diminished her.

To forgive allows the memory of the loss to *shape* what we do with our future but not to *control* what we do. To remember danger keeps us from putting ourselves in dangerous situations in the future. To forgive another person does not mean we subject ourselves to the dangers again. It may simply mean we will move on with our lives without that person's presence in our home.

> *To forgive allows the memory of the loss to shape what we do with our future but not to control what we do.*

Knowing the pain we have been through also creates in us a compassionate spirit for others who are in pain. We do not want to forget the loss or that which has disappeared because it was a part of the life we value—it was a part of the cadre of people who made up who we have become. It is what has made us the interesting person we are.

Forgiveness is not freedom from the memory of the past. It is freedom from the power of what happened in the past. Whether our loss is by choice (I decided to leave her) or by circumstance (he died), guilt will be a part of the loss. We may feel angry at the other person even if they had no power to alter their leaving (if they didn't really choose to die). But the power of that anger and guilt will not have as much control over our future when we have allowed the forgiving spirit to be part of our lives.

This isn't an easy thing to do. We want to be responsible people and we want others to be responsible. It may feel like we are excusing their actions if we allow forgiveness to become part of the fabric of our soul. But forgiveness remembers what happened. It remembers the pain, it remembers the person and their limits and their humanity. It just moves beyond allowing that memory to define how we will live toward that person in the future.

Forgiveness is important because it reminds us the past was not all we needed it to be—and probably could not have been. Mark had to forgive his father. His father did not protect Mark from the pressures of a chaotic life. His father had an addiction that resulted in his being unable to consistently support his son. When his father died, Mark struggled. His anger over the death of his father was compounded by his anger over his father's addiction. Only when Mark was able to remember his dad with all his gifts and graces, along with his pain and inadequacies, was he able to forgive him. Forgiving didn't mean that Mark was excusing his father. It simply meant he didn't allow the pain to distort the full truth about his father.

When Mark was able to forgive his dad, he discovered a new sense of grace in himself toward his own inadequacies. Only when he was freed from the power of his father's mistakes was he able to be less afraid of his own mistakes.

Forgiveness frees up energy for a more adventuresome life. You know you are moving past the pain of the loss when you find you are open to new adventures.

Forgiving others in our lives may require that we explore our relationship to the divine power in the universe. Anger at God is one of the experiences of the spiritual greats of the past. In the ancient scriptures of the Jewish people, there are multiple songs (like Psalm 44) that express their anger at the holy one for not protecting them or for not punishing their enemy. Their anger was a response to God disappointing their sense of justice. Jesus expressed what some believe to be anger at God when he felt deserted at his death. As

> *Anger at God is one of the experiences of the spiritual greats of the past.*

we explore our feelings about losses that seem to be the result of inaction by a divine force who we believe could prevent the loss, we might wonder if a forgiving spirit would be valuable. We may never get to the point of forgiveness, but it is possible to not allow the loss of the past to completely control the way one relates to the universe in the future. When a flood destroys our home, the inability to forgive is understandable. And fear when storms come would be appropriate. But a forgiving spirit is one that is at least open to the sunshine and the grace of spring flowers—even while anger about the flood exists.

Now it is important to remember that these dimensions of processing growth and loss do not always come to us sequentially. There may be days when we are angry, immediately followed by days when we have energy for a creative future. Days of deep sadness and tears may be followed by mellow and poignant days of musing and memory. Forgiveness has a way of weaving itself back and forth through the multiple dimensions of the process.

As we grow toward the new person we are becoming, we will discover we have more energy for the future and spend less and less time remembering the pain and struggle of the past. We will discover we are more anxious to take responsibility for a different

75

future than worrying about what we or others might have done in the past. We will discover that our desire for the future will be accompanied by the strength to make decisions for ourselves without trying to name blame for what happened.

Forgiveness is not something that comes full blown. It comes a bit at a time. Be open to the gift when it comes. Allow it to mellow your heart and release you from the power of the past to control your future.

Good Companions

Notice the people around you who have gone through significant changes in their lives and who seem to have an energy and vitality for living. Go visit them and ask them to tell you about their losses. Ask them to tell you how angry they felt and then how they were freed from the anger. They may have never talked about it, but when you are around these people, you know they have somehow moved beyond the pain to new discoveries and excitement.

Other people who are helpful to you in these times are persons who can mirror back to you your own humanity in a loving way. That is, good friends are people who can help you find humor in your own humanness. They can gently help you see that your moral indignation against another, or against the loss, may be a little over the top and that you, too, share some of the same characteristics of those you judge. When we see in ourselves what we hate in another, we are open to more grace. We can at least see that our future does not depend on remaining attached to the other through our anger at them.

Good friends are also people who can live with us in a way that pulls out of us our past toward a vital future. People who excite our life energy help us realize that the past is just that—past. They help us realize there is life to be lived in the future. Their presence captures our delight and helps us taste the future. Our taste of the future might tease our hunger for something new the way the aroma of freshly baked bread draws us to the kitchen.

7   Gratitude

When one has struggled through the pain and anger of a loss and has allowed the forgiving spirit to begin to do its work, one begins to discover the seventh dimension of the process: *gratitude*. Early in any loss, the intensity of our pain is so profound that we are unable to see the whole picture. We often look at the past through the lens of pain and fear. The person who has been lost is colored by the most intense and most recent experience. But that is not the whole picture. There were other times when there was a larger, more complete picture.

We know that forgiveness of ourselves and others has begun when we can look at the past and find gifts for which we are grateful. Some of what we see is fairly obvious and it is easy to be grateful. When we lose our job at retirement, we can look back on the job and be grateful for the bread and butter it put on our plate and the roof it put over our head. Even if it was not the most satisfying work, it provided something of the necessities of life. We can be grateful for some of the people we knew because they shared our work with us. We can feel grateful that there was some structure to our lives and that we didn't have to make decisions every day about what we were going to do.

Other losses may reveal other gifts that are not so obvious. One of the gifts that came to me when my first wife died was the gift of new eyes with which to see my adult children. I had raised my children, and even though they were young adults, I still treated them as my children. I tried to protect them from the hard things of life—hoping they would not be hurt. I didn't realize I was doing that until I hit a time when I was unable to do it any more. I was so distressed with the losses of my life that I didn't have the energy to protect my children or try to take care of them.

I distinctly remember the day I called each of them and told them I now needed their help. I needed them in some way I was not yet able to articulate. When I admitted my own need and discovered I could not protect them from the pain I was feeling, I discovered what gifted adults they were. They stepped forward and were able to stand by me in my pain, helping me discover truth in my own experience. Because of our loss, we discovered new strength in each other that has served us well in moving toward our own future.

To discover gratitude in the midst of loss does not diminish the value of what is lost. It simply recognizes that there are doors of discovery that open when others are closed. Rose discovered herself alone after thirty-five years of marriage. Her husband died after a long illness. After much struggle, she realized she had been too dependent on her husband for her own identity. She had been known mostly as "Harry's wife." That is the way she had known herself as well. It was very difficult for her after he died. Rose had to learn how to do a lot of things Harry had always done. She had to find a way to support herself. She had to initiate relationship with friends.

> To discover gratitude
> in the midst
> of loss does not
> diminish the value
> of what is lost.

As she moved through the dimensions of growth and grief, she was able to name many of the gifts she had received in his dying. She realized she was a strong woman who could stand by someone in the darkest hour. She realized she was a good partner and that the two of them had had many rich and joyful experiences in their life. Even as she worked through her anger and fear at Harry's dying, Rose's memories filled her with moments of laughter and love.

Rose was able to discover gifts beyond what she had known with Harry. She was able to give thanks for the freedom that was now hers. She could choose to come and go as she pleased. She could travel and explore new places. She could spend the whole weekend in her pajamas. She could try new restaurants that she liked without worrying about Harry. It was not easy for Rose to admit she enjoyed these things. In many ways it felt as if she were happy Harry had died. But she soon was able to see that she was simply celebrating the life she had been given.

The ability to move into gratitude is critical as part of the healing process. It is an important piece in the ability to grow spiritually. For to grow is to embrace reality for what it is, not simply lament because it isn't something else. Everyone loses. Some find joy in the new life they get, while others live in the fear they will be in pain again if they allow themselves to live and love again.

One of the greatest gifts of my life as a pastor was to know people over long periods of time and to discover how they lived their life. Many of the people with whom I worked were over sixty-five. By the time they had lived that long, they had experienced several significant losses. The world had changed, and their own personal tragedies began to pile up.

Some of the people with whom I ministered seemed sad and embittered. They seemed angry that life wasn't the way it had been. They were disappointed that it wasn't all they had hoped it would be. Whenever change was a possibility in the church, they responded with resistance and sometimes anger. One had the feeling that another loss of something that mattered to them would just push them over the edge. It might even push them into deeper bitterness.

There were other people who had experienced a similar series of changes and losses in their lives. But they seemed interested in exploring new things. They looked back on their life and were grateful for what had been, but they somehow allowed that perspective to free them to consider the future as a place for new gifts as well.

I am not sure what the difference between these people was, but it seems as if the former group had never grieved their losses. The pain of that which they had lost seemed to be stuck in their soul like a stone in the shoe and caused them to fear any other change. The latter group remembered their past and were grateful for the gifts it had given to them and were thus open to the gifts that the future might offer as well.

Remember the gifts of pleasure and pain. Each has within it possibilities for a new future. Each has resources for living that will be helpful as you open your heart to the new life that is emerging within you and around you.

Good Companions

Good companions to help you notice and explore this dimension of growth through loss are people who seem to know genuine joy. These are not the people who seem to be perpetually happy and thus oblivious to the fullness of life. These are people who know the struggle but who have sifted through the rubble of their own lives and discovered gifts under the garbage. They are people who feel deeply—who feel pain and pleasure and know that all life is a bit of both.

Good friends are also individuals who will welcome your new discoveries with as much delight as you do. When we have walked around in the wilderness of despair and darkness, some of what we discover as gifts may not shine very brightly to others who have not been where we are. But they are important to us. A good friend is one who finds those gifts to be just as amazing as you do.

During the early years after I left the congregational ministry and started teaching, I lived in constant amazement at the freedom I had. I had lived under the constant demand to preach every seven days. Each week I had to declare myself on something that seemed important to me and to others. Sometimes the pressure was overwhelming. That ritual of preaching was an organizing discipline I missed when I left that ministry, but it was also a gift to be free from having to speak.

As a pastor, I also lived with a to-do list that was never

completed. I went to bed every night with a long list of people to see and books to read and sermons to write. Even when I had a day off to breathe, the to-do list hung around in the back of my mind, weighing down my spirit as it sought to play.

When I became a professor, I discovered that while there were periods of intense work, we had summers off. A whole summer to travel and explore the world. We also had breaks between semesters. And students came into class for fourteen weeks, and then there was a break and we had new students.

I was amazed at the possibility of having a life less structured by the demands of the job. I shared the delight with my new friends who had been living this life. It seemed normal to them. But they patiently listened to me as I went on about the joy of this freedom.

As you journey through your pilgrimage of loss, find people who can share your delight. When you speak your gratitude, it becomes more real. When gratitude is shared, it has a longer life.

Find persons to write to—even if it is to yourself. Either through letters or journals, find ways of writing about your gifts. Express your delight and joy in the life you shared with the one you lost, as well as the discoveries you are making about yourself and the world because you no longer have that relationship. Both are gifts for which one can be thankful. When you write them down, they become more visible, and when you share them, others can remind you of their presence in those times when you might forget. When you write them in a journal, you can return to them when clouds descend in your soul and you feel there is nothing worth living for. These discoveries will feed you when you are hungry for hope.

Play

T o learn to live again as a new person after one has lost important parts of who they are requires the ability to play again. You will know you are moving more into the world of the new self when you sense you are playing with new ways of doing things. To play is to live out a new way of life within the safety of uncommitted space.

The play of children is the way they grow and become new and different people. When my son was three years old, he would get in my closet and pull down a shirt and tie of mine. He would put the shirt on with the tail dragging the floor. He would tie a knot in the tie and put it around his neck. He put on my sneakers and stumbled around the house pretending to be grown up. He was trying on what it was like to be a man. He was able to pretend without the responsibility. This is the way children grow into new and different ways of being in the world. They look at adults and then pretend to cook in the kitchen or teach in the classroom.

When we have had a significant loss, we not only lose our partner, our home, our job, or our child. We lose our identity. We mourn the loss not only of the other, but of ourselves in relation to the other. To become something other than what we have been requires that we try on new clothes.

When a student graduates from college, she is often uncertain of her identity. She has a degree, but what will she do with it? It is not at all unusual for her to try on several jobs when she first graduates. These are ways of playing with who she sees herself becoming. If she is single and does not have responsibility for family or friends, she has the freedom to try different jobs. It is hard to know who we are becoming unless we have a chance to try on different identities.

If we have been married and find ourselves single again, we date. Dating is a way of seeing who we are becoming. It allows us to feel and see what is within us that is alive. Dating is as much a way of finding what we want to be within ourselves as it is finding someone who we can love. Because who we love shapes who we become, the presence of the other person helps us know what we want to be. We grow to love not only the other person, but love what we become when we are with them. We play our way into new ways of being and living. Dating different people helps us discover different dimensions of ourselves and therefore imagine becoming a new person.

To grow spiritually is to imagine ourselves as different kinds of people. It is to play with different ways of being in the world. I have come to imagine this growth by seeing the self as composed of four quadrants. We know ourselves by the voices we listen to from within each of those quadrants. Imagine a large X (see Illustration 3). In the quadrant on the left are the voices from our past. They are the voices of parents and teachers, family and mentors who have helped shape our values. The voices in the top quadrant are voices from the contemporary world. They are the voices of news, advertisement, music, our children, our boss, and others with whom we live whose presence shapes what we do with our time. The voices in the bottom

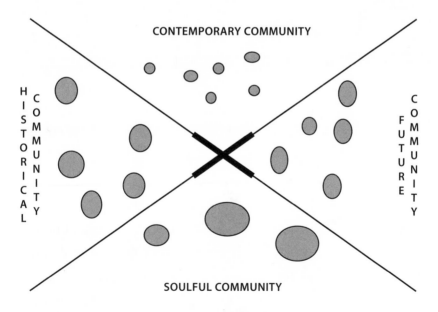

Illustration 3

quadrant are voices of the soul. These are the whispering voices of conscience, intuition, and emotion. This reflects our unique way of responding to our world and is what we most value and fear. The voices in the quadrant on the right are voices of the future. These are a combination of the imagination and offers that the future extends to us. They whisper and seduce us toward them, giving us activities to live for tomorrow.

Most of us live our lives by paying attention to the voices closest to the center of the X (see Illustration 4). We listen to voices that create a balanced circle that reinforces what we know ourselves to be. We try to create equilibrium by listening to the voices that create the most peace for us. For example, if we are

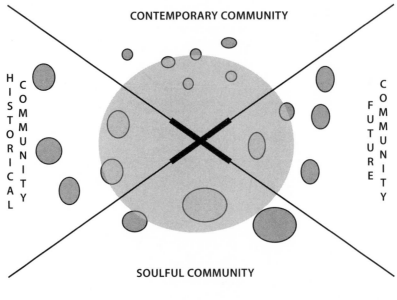

Illustration 4

married and with family, we listen to voices from our past that tell us that we are to be responsible and faithful to this family. We then listen to people within the contemporary world of voices who help us do that. We listen to our soul's values that nurture that activity. And we plan activities for tomorrow that will serve our goal of being responsible and faithful to our family. We generally try to quiet the voices in the four quadrants that would seduce us into being unfaithful to those responsibilities. Our lives have some balance and we are able to function to produce the desired effect.

When a crisis occurs, the balanced circle in the center of the X spins out of control and an imbalance is created. It is like a round balloon filled with air. If you just let it go and let the air come out, it flies crazy-like here and there. It creates chaos. There is no straight line, but a scattering, spinning dance in the sky (see Illustration 5). For example, if you lose your job, everything in the circle is threatened. Your ability to be responsible as you know responsibility is threatened. The voices of your boss and the people at your work are no longer the dominant voices in the contemporary world. Suddenly you are listening to other voices in the quadrant—voices that might offer another way of being responsible. The voices of your soul that speak to you of your self-doubt—voices that might have been silenced as you were functioning capably in your previous job—begin to cry out and anxiety sets in. And suddenly the voices from your future that invite you to consider a new career begin to sound more interesting.

Growth occurs when you begin to pay attention to voices out-

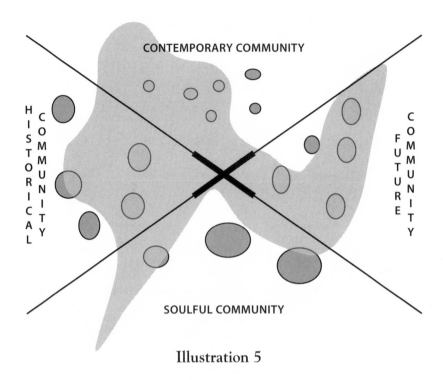

Illustration 5

side the comfortable circle of balance and equilibrium. When we begin to play with other ways of living our lives, we create the opportunity for growth.

This isn't simply the way we create growth when there has been a loss. It is the way we grow in all our life.

To be alive is to need both stability and adventure, predictability and surprise. We need to pay attention to the familiar and ordered voices of our familiar communities. We need to know that we belong and to feel the safety of routine and ritual. But if we are really alive, we also need the adventure of strange voices.

We need the challenge of being around the exotic and unusual voices of strangers who live life in very different ways.

If we live only with the comfortable and familiar, we can become lethargic and dull. If we live only with the strange and adventuresome, we will feel chaotic and disordered. To be a growing and living creature, we rest with the familiar voices and play with the strange ones. That balance can contribute to a stable and adventuresome life.

It is important to remember that play requires grace. When we play, we make mistakes. When we are uncertain about who we are and our own strengths and weaknesses, we will make mistakes. We will, in many ways feel like little children.

> *If we are really alive, we need the adventure of strange voices.*

Ron had worked hard and was lucky. He had been able to accumulate enough material wealth to retire at fifty-three. He was excited. No longer did he have to punch a time clock. He didn't have to be accountable to the company. He was free. When he retired, however, he reported he felt scared in his freedom. He said he felt like a child learning to walk. He said he would try to figure out what to do with his day and he was uncertain if he was doing what he should. Forgiveness and grace are very important when one is playing in new and unfamiliar territory. We must have the freedom to make mistakes without becoming our mistakes if we are going to become new and different people.

You know you are moving toward becoming a new person when the spirit of play returns to your life. You may even discover you don't want play to be absent in your new life and that you want to open up to a life of spiritual growth and discovery, expanding your world of memory, of presence, of soul, and the future by making decisions to risk losing old ways of being to explore new ways of living.

Good Companions

Good companions for this dimension of your experience are people who do not depend on your listening to only those voices in the safe circle. They are people who can allow you to try on new clothes without judging you as silly.

For example, if you do not know how to dance, it is good to be around people who do not laugh at you for trying. You need people around you who can accept the idea that you may change your mind about what you value and how you want to spend your time. You need people who can listen to you as you imagine what you might look like living a different way.

One of the best friends I had during my time of discovery is the person who became my wife. Deborah and I were experiencing many of the same feelings, living in the chaos of trying to figure out who we were going to be since the worlds we had lived in collapsed around us. We didn't need the other person to be something for us because we didn't know what that other person had to offer. As we discovered each other, we realized that neither of us knew the person who had lived in the past. We only knew what we or others told us about our past.

For example, Deborah didn't know that I had spent thirty years of my life in a suit and tie. The only way she had known me was in jeans and sweatshirts. She didn't know that I had enjoyed a disciplined life of office and home. She only knew me as one who wandered the planet, following my impulses to travel and explore the world.

When we are playing with new possibilities in becoming new selves, it is good to have individuals around us who can simply delight in who we are now and who do not need us to be what we were.

This, of course, is hard to do. Most of us live in social systems that limit our relationships with strangers. If we are a couple who has been married twenty-five years and our children leave the house, it is very difficult to change the way we relate. Each has become so familiar with the patterned habits of the other that it is frightening to consider that the other person might make some changes.

And yet it is that fresh and new that creates excitement and adventure. Many marriages have trouble when the children leave home. The couple does not know how to be with each other in a new way. When this occurs, it is important for each spouse to have opportunity to explore new friendships and new hobbies that will help them become new. As the individuals in the marriage take on new dimensions, the marriage will have the potential to take on new dimensions.

Another kind of friend that is helpful in these times is a friend that comes to you through books. Books are rich with people who live life in different ways, and these stories can trigger your imagination. In your mind you can play with new *possibilities. You can talk about them with people around you. You can play in your mind long before you try things in your life. When you do try something different, it will not be like you imagined, but at least the imagination helps you prepare for what might be different.*

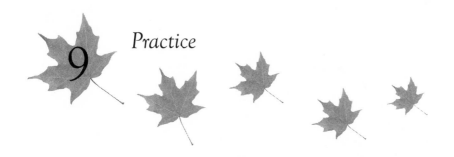

Practice

A ninth dimension discovered by those who are growing through grieving is that of *practice*. After we have explored a variety of options for living again, somewhere along the way we will discover that some options represent who we are more than others. When we come to that awareness, we begin practicing those options more than others. If you are dating and discover that one man helps you know yourself the way you want to know yourself, then you spend more time with him. If we are exploring different jobs, eventually we come to a point where one job satisfies more than another and we settle into that job.

I was a pastor in three congregations. I was a pastor for thirty years. When I was unable to continue in congregational leadership, I was called to be a professor. Resetting my trajectory after thirty years, I had to spend time exploring what it meant. I had to imagine how to be in the seminary. I spent large chunks of

> *Without any decision, it is hard to commit ourselves to doing that which brings new life.*

time wandering the country in my car, watching how others lived their lives and talking with strangers. Over time it became clear that the role of professor was more satisfying for me than other options.

The first thing we must do when we feel we want to become the person we imagine ourselves to be is to decide—to make a choice. This, of course, is often difficult because it means we will lose other options. We are working through one loss, and then as we settle on a particular choice, we cut ourselves off from other options. Without any decision, however, it is hard to commit ourselves to doing that which brings new life.

Once I made the decision that I wanted to be a professor, I worked at practicing the art of teaching. I had to cut myself off from the other choices I might have made and only practice teaching. It is the discipline of practice that creates the difference between one who plays the piano and one who is a pianist. It is the discipline of writing that makes the difference between writing and being a writer. It is committing oneself to the art of drawing that makes the difference between one who draws and an artist.

What happens at this point in the process of growing through grieving is that we allow our love for what we are becoming to shape how we spend our time. When a child is born into the family, we lose the life we had before she was born. By virtue of the birth, we are called parents. But most of us begin this process stumbling around, wondering if we really are parents and if we can actually be parents. As we commit ourselves to the child we love and as we practice the skills, acting and making mistakes and learning from those mistakes and acting again, we eventually become the role we are playing.

As we spend more time living the role we are learning, we often grow in our love for it. To *fall in love* with a new way of being and to *love* that way of being are two different things. Sarah fell in love with the idea of being a teacher. She was drawn to it because she enjoyed the teachers she'd had as a student. She enjoyed the exploration of ideas and the adventure of discovery.

When Sarah became a teacher, however, the enchantment wore off. She came to understand that what had drawn her to teaching was the experience of being a student. When she learned that teaching required more than simply exploring ideas, she wondered about her choice. She struggled with all the paperwork required by the administration. She lost sleep over the parent/teacher conferences where parents became defensive for their children. She worked to try to keep up her energy as she graded papers into the night.

Even so, the more Sarah worked at teaching, the more she became a teacher. She discovered that loving teaching and learning kept her focused on what was required to ensure that the students had a chance to know the excitement of learning that she had known.

When the time comes on the journey of learning to live a new

> *Many of us are so anxious to live that we miss the living that is going on within us.*

life, make a decision and begin to practice it. Obviously the commitment may lead you to the awareness that you do not really want to pursue that way of being, but until a commitment is made, the full impact of the new direction will not be known.

When Deborah and I were dating, we struggled to determine how committed we wanted to be. We dated, got close, and then were scared off. We then did not see each other for several months before we tried it again. And again, when we dated that second time, we began to bump up against resistances within ourselves that pushed us apart. Eventually we decided we liked ourselves better together than separate—so we committed to our love. We practiced that love and stayed together through the hard parts. This eventually led us to a marriage commitment.

Now as any of you who have lived in a committed relationship know, what it looks like from the outside is different from what it is on the inside. We committed ourselves to love and cherish each other. It is the practice of that commitment, though, which brings about the new life of cherished love.

To grow spiritually requires similar practice. It requires the practice of paying attention—of slowing down and noticing what is going on around you and within you. Many of us are so anxious to live that we miss the living that is going on within us. We are so eager to know more and do more that we miss what is happening right around us. To grow spiritually is to be open to the moving of the creative energy in the life within and around us.

Paying attention requires intentionality. It requires that we get off the interstates and fast trains and travel the scenic routes. Some people find meditation or centering prayer helpful in this task. These practices are disciplines that we do even when we feel we don't have the time or desire to do them. We stop for twenty or thirty minutes and close our eyes, breathing in the air around us. We relax our muscles into the chair and allow ourselves to be held. We slow down the chaos of our minds, focusing on some scene or word that quiets the anxiety of the soul. We notice our own heartbeat, our own blood coursing through our veins, our own skin as it is teased by our hair. We notice life within us, allowing the barriers of speed and noise to fade away. With this practice, the quiet voices within have a chance to whisper their longings and we get to know ourselves better.

The consequence of paying attention is that we begin to slow down and notice the world around as well. We begin to discover there is a giftedness in simply being—that we don't need more things or more activities—but life is already here as a gift to us. We notice the gifts which have been ours and which are ours now. We remember the moments of change and new life that have come to us in the past.

Other people practice paying attention by journaling. They take time every day to write the life they notice around themselves and within themselves. They notice the small things. One discipline which helps is to remember the most insignificant thing that happened to you today and then reflect on it. It's easy to think of the important or big things that might have occurred, but when you try to think of the most inconsequential thing that happened, you have to reflect on almost everything. You have to take notice of the life that is yours. What happens is that you discover life in the most unexpected places.

Deciding and then practicing the new life you are discovering is one of the things that happens on the way to becoming new.

Good Companions

One of the hard parts of this dimension in our journey toward newness is discovering people who can help us stay focused on our new life. Most of us are part of social systems that have a stake in our getting back to normal; they are not interested in having to adapt so we can be different. It requires a strong person with good social support to develop new ways of responding to the world around us. Therefore one of the most important things we can watch for in our journey toward the future is individuals who can help us practice the new life.

This means we need persons who can hear what we like about who we are becoming and who can hold us accountable to the vision we have for ourselves. I discovered that some counselors are very good at this. As I was working on finding a new way and becoming more comfortable with the absence of many things that had made me who I was, I discovered a counselor who walked with me. One of his primary tasks was to remember who I was from week to week and gently remind me of it when I went to see him. When we are alone in the world and making our way, we are living in social systems that want us to be what they need for us to be. When someone walks with us and helps us remember who we are becoming, we are more able to practice that new way of living.

Coaches are also good at this. In sports, coaches have a way of holding players accountable to the disciplines that help them become the kind of pitcher or quarterback they want to be. It is often easy to give in to old patterns that are not effective in improving one's skills, and a coach helps a player stay focused on the best disciplines for better results.

There are business and life coaches whose purpose is the same thing. They listen carefully to us and help us understand what it is we are becoming. They then visit with us with some regularity, asking us questions to keep us focused on what we said we wanted to become. They help us consider and establish disciplines that we believe will produce the kind of person we want to be, and then they remind us of those disciplines each time we visit with them. Coaches and counselors can be invaluable in our effort to grow the new dimensions which are emerging within us.

Other companions that help us in this task of practicing the new self are people who have had some success in becoming more effective in being who they desire to be. I have discovered writers who are effective in communicating the way I want to. I have visited with them and read books by them on what they do to make it possible to produce written material.

When it comes to the loss of ourselves by the loss of someone who was significant to us, it is good to be with other people who have experienced similar losses and have become new. Wilma lost a child to an accident when the child was only five years old. She didn't think she would ever be able to live again—the best she would be able to do was survive each day *without collapsing into chaos. And for many months that is about all she could do—put one foot in front of the other and hope it would hold her up. But after about a year, she found a group of people who were all grieving the loss of a child. Some of them had a more recent loss than hers. Others had lost children ten years earlier. Walking along with these people, Wilma discovered there were things she could do to think beyond the next moment. She learned by being with those who had lived ten years after their loss that there is hope to live. She didn't always believe it and it was very difficult, but she began the ritual of attending the meetings and also the practice of getting out with other people.*

Wilma is living today. She has a way of life that has some of the same dimensions to it as did her life before her loss. She is finding some moments of laughter and even glimpses of joy. By forcing herself into certain disciplines of community, she has begun to see herself as a woman who has lost a child rather than simply a childless mother.

Good friends whose presence reminds us of who we want to become are invaluable as we move toward the new self we are becoming.

10 *Becoming New*

B ecoming a new creation is not something that you do—it is something that happens to you. It is like being born. You didn't do anything—it was a gift to you. The tenth experience of this growing-through-grieving process is a kind of birthing into a new life.

It comes when you least expect it. It comes in fits and starts. There will be moments when you feel comfortable being in your skin. The driving energy you once had to run from your fears and fill your life with frenetic activity seems to have dissipated. You find you can sit and rest—sink into the present moment and accept the grace of it. This may not happen for years, but when you get here, you will have become someone who knows joy.

We know we are at this point in the process when we feel like a child again. That is, when we are as open to what is around us as a newborn. Rebirth is not coming to some way of being that you choose. It is like an infant who is awake and open to all that is around her. An infant is one who has not been conditioned to define some things as good and some things as bad. She is simply open to tasting and seeing, touching and discovering. We know we are becoming new when our senses and desires are awake and alive.

My experience with the grieving process has taught me that this experience happens to us—it is not something we can create in ourselves. It comes to us when we have felt our pain and that pain has become integrated into who we are, not a barrier to new experiences. It comes to us when we have remembered well what was lost and remembered long enough that it no longer defines us but simply informs who we are. It comes to us when we have experienced the grace of forgiveness, no longer being haunted by the guilt of what might have been and was not, or what was not that might have been. It comes to us when we feel strong enough to play again—to explore the larger world of strangers. It comes to us when we develop our new discoveries and find our love and our life in them.

> *We know we are becoming new when our senses and desires are awake and alive.*

When this comes, it doesn't mean we will forget the past. The past with all its pain and pleasure will have a bittersweet quality to it. We will remember it as a source of understanding of who we are and who we are becoming. The threads of memory, tinged with tears and thanksgiving, have woven themselves into a comforter, wrapping us and warming us on cold winter nights.

When we awake one day and realize we are actually living into the present in a natural and relaxed way, not really working at it but letting it open us up to the world within and around us, we will feel a new joy and contentment. Because we feel more secure in who we have become, we can better integrate the past, present, and future. The becoming of a new self is the awareness that who we have been, who we are, and who we are becoming are no longer in painful struggle with each other. We feel whole. There will certainly be moments when emptiness will cause us to feel fractured and broken, but much of the time we will find a measure of peace.

No one can say when this gift will come. It is usually a surprise. It comes in those moments when we feel at home in our own skin. It isn't some constant state of well-being. That kind of experience is utopia (no place). Expecting a state of nirvana is to always be disappointed. But there will be more moments of awareness that we are alive and that life is good and worth living and sharing.

To be born anew in the spirit is to be alive to the living, creative spirit that breathes and moves around us. We will know the gift of rebirth has come to us when we are able to simply be awake and see the creative love of the divine in the human and created world around us. We will have moments of delight, when our desires and our experiences marry and light shimmers in our hearts.

Good Companions

The best companions when you are experiencing this dimension of the process are those people with whom you feel at home. These are the individuals you have met along the way who like the new person who has been born. They are folks who know how to celebrate with you as you discover joy again.

And they are people who may or may not have known you before your loss. If they are persons who have known you before and have been able to walk with you through your journey, you are doubly blessed. For they not only share the dreams of your future, but they share the memories of your past. They will not only be there to walk with you in the adventure of discovering a new world, but they will be able to sit by the fire with you and remember the rich gifts of who you were before.

If the people who are companions with you at this point are new and only a part of your life since the loss, then you are richly blessed. For they are respectful enough of your past, which they do not know, to trust that you are who you are today because of who you have been. They have grace to accept what they do not know because it is a mystery that has brought them the person that they do know.

It is very important that the people we walk with are those who find delight in us. For us to delight in ourselves, it is good to have people around us who enjoy us. The new person we have become is integrating into a new community of people who will share and celebrate that new life.

Epilogue: What Matters Most

T o live is to love. To love is to lose. To lose is to live.

So where do we go from here? How do we attend to these multiple dimensions of growing and grieving? How do we stay present to the life we have and discover new life that is being born within us?

I'm not sure, but there are a few hints that might give us some clues. I was raised in a religious home with strict guidelines about behavior and belief. The stability created by a family and social system that reinforced the beliefs was reassuring as well as stifling. Knowing what I believed helped me act with some degree of confidence.

When I went away to college, however, I lost the social system that helped me maintain my stabilizing center. The expanding world of knowledge and the discovery that other people found different lifestyles just as satisfying as I found mine caused me to question all I held to be true and sacred. That questioning drilled through my mind and heart down into the very bone marrow of my soul. I was in not only a faith crisis but a life crisis.

Two people helped me discover a different center to help me through the grieving process of learning to live again. The first was Bill Stringfellow, an attorney who had given up a lucrative law practice to work with the poor in Harlem. He was the speaker at an international youth conference I attended. Early in the week I had been on a boat ride on Lake Geneva in Wisconsin and remember standing at the rear of the boat alone, looking down at the churning water. The black, cold chaos of the lake seemed much calmer than the terrifying chaos of my heart and soul. I was tempted to join the water.

I went to visit Mr. Stringfellow. I don't remember anything he said to me. But I do remember receiving a package in the mail a few weeks after I returned to my campus in Oklahoma. It was from Mr. Stringfellow. I opened it and out fell a little book, *Mr. Blue*, by Myles Connolly. It was a novel about an attorney who had given up a lucrative law practice to serve the poor. In the fly of the book, Bill had written the following, "Few people know how few things really matter. Mr. Blue."

That book arriving in my life at that time contributed to my ability to let some of the structure and stability of my life go. It helped me begin to focus on the question: What really matters? Much of what I was clinging to in order to stay afloat was mere flotsam. I needed to grieve the loss of the world I had known. I needed to open myself to the few things that mattered most for my moving ahead. But what were they?

In my quest to discover the answer to that question, I visited one of my professors. Dr. Roger Carstensen taught Old Testament. I remember telling Dr. Carstensen that I didn't believe anything anymore. I was frightened and losing myself.

Dr. Carstensen then asked me a question: "Do you believe anything at all?"

I thought a while and finally said, "Well, I believe that love is better than not love."

To which he said, "Faith is like a bicycle. You have to be moving to get your balance. So if you believe in love, ride love."

Those two encounters with people who cared enough to take me seriously and give me the benefit of their wisdom laid the groundwork for my whole life. And I believe they lay the foundation for what matters the most when it comes to grieving loss. Riding love is the way to rediscover life through loss.

What does it mean to love? I have come to believe that love is paying attention. When you love someone, you notice them. You pay attention to them. You engage them with your senses and your dreams and they become important to you even as they shape who you are. To ride love through life is to pay attention to your life, its pain and pleasure, its joy and sorrow.

But what do we love? If only a few things really matter, what are they? As one who has found Jesus a helpful companion for life, I look to his answer. When some smart people asked him what the way to life was, he said to love God, love neighbor, and love self with all you are—heart, mind, body, and soul. That is the way of life. Pay careful attention to what is created, the environment, the neighbor, and the self. If you pay attention to this life in its multiple forms, you not only gain strength from the many relationships you have, but you gain insight into how to live the life you have been given. Learning to grieve, learning to live again in the absence of something significant, isn't a matter of simply getting through some preordained process. It is a matter of living fully the life you have been given as you go through it.

To love the created order, to love the neighbor, and to love the self is to pay attention to all that is around you—to slow down and take notice of it—not to judge it but to see what is in it that can nourish your energy for life.

I have discovered the creation around me is filled with moments of delight and inspiration even as it is replete with terror and destruction. The problem is usually that I am so busy with all the things that matter that I fail to notice.

I was hiking in the woods recently. The trees were naked and the snow lay freshly fallen on the path. But I had important things to do. I had to get my heartbeat up so that I could do my aerobic exercise. I was also pondering the next chapter of the book I was writing. I was oblivious to all that was around me. Then suddenly there was a bolt off to my right. Hair standing up on the back of my neck, I stopped still to stare. And there, only fifty yards to the right, was a beautiful deer—standing still, staring at me. My heart quieted as we just stared at each other. Here was creation, all around me, and I almost missed it. So I slowed down as I walked on and looked at the corduroy patterns across the path as the sun shadowed through the trees. I sucked in air that was cold, crisp. I allowed myself to wake up to the world around me and was grateful for the sustaining environment with all its grace.

To love creation is not only to notice, but it is also to allow oneself to be nourished by it. Deborah and I were driving through wine country in northern California. We had never been there before and we were reveling in the fertile soil and the "teddy bear" hills that rolled out ahead and behind us. We were enjoying each other and were open to the sunlight when it suddenly turned dark. We had driven into the cathedral forest of redwood trees. And towering above us were these ancient specimens of the creative hand. I pulled the car over and Deborah got out of the car. I will never forget watching her walk over to one of the trees and gently place her hands on the bark and begin to weep—overwhelmed with awe at the creative life around us.

When we are broken and vulnerable, struggling to figure out who we are in the absence of someone or something that is significant, it is good to slow down and take notice of the beauty and grace around us. Even the storms can serve as a reminder of the power of the unpredictable and can echo the chaos within our own souls. Even in the thunder and lightning of a summer storm, we can feel we are not alone in our own stormy soul.

If we are to love what God creates, then we pay attention to not only the nature that is around us, but we love our neighbor as well. There are people, familiar and stranger, who inhabit all our worlds. And they are people who have value and whose perspective on life is worth our listening to. Be fully present to them.

This is not always easy. For we sometimes ignore our neighbor because they are not who we want them or need for them to be. We often miss noticing the real person because we are blinded by the person we have created them to be.

My mother has lost much of her memory. It is not easy to visit her because I don't know what to say or do. For the first ninety-one years of her life, her memory was sharp as a tack. She loved engaging issues and arguing her position. Now she cannot do that. And even while I am happy to get to "be" right now, I miss my mother. I miss her because the person I knew is not there.

On a recent visit, Deborah suggested we take some hymns for my mother to listen to. (My mother was a church organist for many years and loves church music.) Deborah downloaded the hymns onto a disk. We packed up my boom box and drove the five hundred miles to visit Mother. When we got there, we saw her watching the little children who were playing at the day care center outside the window of her nursing center. We sat with her and while we didn't visit much, we shared her delight in the children. She waved and laughed and pointed, celebrating the child in her as she watched the children around her.

Later we went into her room and set up the CD player. We put on the CD and began to listen to some of the great hymns of the church—"A Mighty Fortress Is Our God," "Immortal, Invisible," "Great Is Thy Faithfulness," "How Great Thou Art." And I sat there watching my mother, eyes gazing at the ceiling, her fingers fluctuating between a steepled prayer and playing the organ. I heard her mouth a few of the words she could remember. And

I wept. For an hour, surrounded by my mother's music, my wife's grace, and pictures of my father and siblings, I wept.

I didn't want to make this visit. I had important things to do. My mother was no longer there. And I almost missed my neighbor. I almost missed her because she was not who I remembered her to be or wanted her to be. But had I not been there, had I not had my ego slowed down and embraced by her music, I would have missed the glimpse of my mother as a child, my mother as a poetic spirit whose soul had nurtured and cared for my soul, and who had helped shape me into who I am.[5]

To love our neighbor is to pay them our attention. It is to intentionally allow their gifts—as inadequate and as broken as they might feel—to embrace us. When we are frightened and lonely and struggling with our pain, sometimes we receive gifts from the most unlikely places. When we feel alone, sometimes it is the most wounded and scarred among us who has the ability to be present with us in ways that offer healing to our hearts.

What matters most in our lives is to pay attention to them. It is to live our lives—to notice ourselves and the world around us. It is to be awake to each moment, trusting that in the moment there will be something that will offer possible hope and healing.

But loving what is created also includes loving ourselves. And for many people, this is one of the most difficult things to do. Many have been taught to pay attention to others and often end up ignoring their own needs. We have been taught not to be selfish, and some of us were taught to put others' needs above our own.

But loving ourselves—paying attention to our own feelings and desires—is not selfishness. It is realizing that creation has offered us this gift of life and the best thing we can do is to care for it in a way that allows it to live and bless others. It is hard to give ourselves to others if we do not have a self to give.

I have come to believe that self-love is not the problem in the world. It is self-loathing that is the problem. People who love themselves are people who rejoice in their own existence. They are people who are strong in their own self-understanding. People who hate themselves are the people who put others down so they will feel better about themselves. People who do not like who they are will spend all their time trying to make themselves likable. They will spend all their money trying to buy the things that will make other people like or love them. They will be easily manipulated by religious or secular leaders who want to control what they do with their lives. Self-love is discovering the gift of life you are and nurturing that gift for the sake of all of creation.

As we grieve loss and grow toward a new life, we often fail to attend to our own needs. We believe people who tell us to press on and get over it. We are often driven by our fear to stay busy so that we won't have to feel the fear. The vacancy at the table is so achingly lonely we can hardly stand it, so we keep having people over to fill the chair.

But to be alive and to love ourselves requires that we take some time just paying attention to what we are feeling and doing. In paying attention to our weariness, we might feel free to give into it and take a rest. We may change our lives for a while to adapt to the energy it takes to rediscover our world. When I left the parish ministry and moved into the seminary, I was so exhausted with all the losses of my life that I took a nap every day in my office—lying on the floor with my feet on the chair and my head on my rolled-up jacket. To love yourself is to attend to your need in the changing landscape of your soul's journey.

As you live your life—as you live the new life that is emerging out of the chaos of your loss—love creation, neighbor, and self. Pay attention to what is happening around you. Notice how different you feel and discover gifts in that difference. Share your journey with strangers and friends, allowing them to offer their gifts of presence and understanding. Listen to all the new voices rising within you. Let them be heard with the other voices as well.

When you do, you may discover a new self emerging within you. You may discover that there is life beyond the loss even as that life was revealed through the loss. And you may even find glimpses of peace along the way.

Endnotes

1. Susan Ford Wiltshire, *Seasons of Grief and Grace: A Sister's Story of AIDS* (Nashville: Vanderbilt University Press, 1995).

2. Wiltshire, *Seasons of Grief and Grace.*

3. Jack Gilbert, "Tear It Down." *The Great Fires: Poems 1982–1992* (New York: Alfred A. Knopf, 2000), 9.

4. Milan Kundera, *Immortality* (New York: Harper Perennial, 1991), 223.

5. My mother died August 31, 2007, during the publishing process of this book. The gift of her spirit that came through this experience of poetry and music will continue to sustain me.

Recommended Reading

On my journey through loss, the following books have been my good friends. In their own unique way they have given me a sense that I am not alone and that dark days are not only followed by brighter ones, but that there are gifts in the darkness.

Annie Dillard, *Pilgrim at Tinker Creek*

Barbara A. Holmes, *Joy Unspeakable: Contemplative Practices of the Black Church*

Barbara Brown Taylor, *When God is Silent*

Belden Lane, *The Solace of Fierce Landscapes: Exploring Desert and Mountain Spirituality*

David Whyte, *The Heart Aroused: Poetry and the Preservation of the Soul in Corporate America*

RECOMMENDED READING

Diane Ackerman, *A Natural History of the Senses*

Esther de Waal, *Living With Contradiction: An Introduction to Benedictine Spirituality*

Jerry Sittser, *A Grace Disguised: How the Soul Grows through Loss*

Mary Jane Moffat, ed., *In the Midst of Winter*

Phil Cousineau, *The Art of Pilgrimage: The Seeker's Guide to Making Travel Sacred*

Renita J. Weems, *Listening for God: A Minister's Journey Through Silence and Doubt*

Simone Weil, *Waiting for God*

Susan Ford Wiltshire, *Seasons of Grief and Grace: A Sister's Story of AIDS*

Thomas Attig, *How We Grieve: Relearning the World*

Wendy Farley, *The Wounding and Healing of Desire: Weaving Heaven and Earth*

William Bridges, *Transitions: Making Sense of Life's Changes*